AFTER
THE
STORM

Joseph Sommers is an associate professor of Romance languages at the University of Washington, Seattle. He has published numerous studies on Mexican prose fiction in both Mexico and the United States. His book on Francisco Rojas González, a writer of the revolutionary period, was published in 1966 by the Universidad Veracruzana. He was assisted in preparing the present work by a grant from the Joint Committee on Latin American Studies of the ACLS and the SSRC.

This drawing was done especially for this book by Jose Luis Cuevas.

AFTER THE STORM

Landmarks of the Modern Mexican Novel

Joseph Sommers

University of
New Mexico
Press

© THE UNIVERSITY OF NEW MEXICO PRESS, 1968. ALL RIGHTS RE-
SERVED. Manufactured in the United States of America by The University
of New Mexico Printing Plant, Albuquerque. *Library of Congress Catalog
Card No. 68-23019. First edition.*

For Tish & Bill:

Modern man likes to pretend that his thinking is wide-awake. But this wide-awake thinking has led us into the mazes of a nightmare in which the torture chambers are endlessly repeated in the mirrors of reason. When we emerge, perhaps we will realize that we have been dreaming with our eyes open, and that the dreams of reason are intolerable. And then, perhaps, we will begin to dream once more with our eyes closed.

—Octavio Paz

CONTENTS

PREFACE

THE LAST TEN YEARS have witnessed the publication in English translation of Mexico's outstanding contemporary novelists—Augustín Yáñez, Juan Rulfo, and Carlos Fuentes. Each author has received favorable but necessarily brief reviews in such periodicals as *The New York Times* and *The New Yorker*. The present study, aimed at reinforcing this beachhead of Mexican letters on the American scene, is addressed to three types of readers: those with a general interest in the modern novel, who would be concerned with more ample critical studies in order to see Mexican fiction both in depth and in perspective; those many Americans with a broad background in Mexican cultural life; and lastly, students of Latin American literature—for even in scholarly texts and academic journals there has been a dearth of serious critical evaluation of these modern writers.

An operating premise here is that the Mexican novel reaches a new level of maturity beginning with the publication in 1947 of *The Edge of the Storm (Al filo del agua)* by Agustín Yáñez. This notion has been stated in general terms by critics such as Emmanuel Carballo and authors like Carlos Fuentes. The effort in the pages which follow, however, is to substantiate the premise in critical terms and relate it to the present status of the novel, as seen from the vantage point of 1967.

The initial chapter examines "the novel of the Revolution"—a movement which began in 1915 and lasted some three decades. Three of its most representative creations are treated, in the inseparable context of the nationalism which the Revolution engendered. Succeeding sections deal individually with the four landmark novels which mark the stages of development since 1947. The term landmark is used in the sense that each work represents a significant new advance in literary expression. Chapter VI, based on the premise that the new novel is indeed a genuine movement, a stage beyond an accidental succession of outstanding writers, delves into the literary context of the novels by Yáñez, Rulfo, and Fuentes. Its aim is to measure various tendencies in prose fiction, especially in the years from 1955 to 1964. The important novels produced by a growing number of significant writers are discussed briefly in order to attain an overview of the literary and intellectual environment from which the major works emerged.

The concluding chapter seeks a tentative assessment of the modern novel, addressing itself to a series of questions: What are the literary merits and the significance of the landmark works? How are these merits different from those of the novel of the Revolution? What techniques and forms typify the new novel? Is there a composite cosmovision, a shared perspective from which these authors view Mexico and the world? Can new directions or a new phase be discerned in the immediate future? What problems have been created for the talented generation of authors now coming upon the scene?

The aim is not to produce a volume of literary history

—a goal admirably attained by John S. Brushwood. His recent study, *Mexico In Its Novel*,[1] organizes into a coherent sequence of periods and thematic tendencies the vast amount of narrative fiction produced in the century and a half since the birth of the Mexican novel in 1816, with the publication of *El Periquillo Sarniento* by José Joaquín Fernández de Lizardi. The present effort is rather to define the major contours of the modern novel. The approach is to select the principle authors who are responsible for these contours, and to study in some depth their major works to date. By charting the conceptual breadth and the formal dimensions, it is possible to set out the distinctive literary features which the modern novel has acquired in Mexico.

There are a number of assumptions implicit in this approach. One is that literary criticism is an indispensable complement to literary history. In fact, each area blends into the other. Most historians of Mexican literature will venture the critical estimate that Yáñez, Rulfo and Fuentes have been the most significant novelists of recent decades. But the basis for this judgment can be authenticated only by the kind of study which does not fit into a history of literature, that is, by a study of the major achievements by each author. Hopefully the present volume will be convincing enough to justify the prior literary judgments which dictated its organization.

A second premise which underlies this study is that the novelist is somehow connected with history, that by channels of intuition, psychology or spirit he participates in his times. Paradoxically, however, the extent to which he respects his craft, treating the novel as an autonomous creation, is the degree to which he may convey indirectly a significant interpretive commentary on his times. In order to evaluate, then, a primary consideration is artistic authenticity. From the very texture of form and technique emerges the artist's personal structure of values. In other words, if *War and Peace* reflects the spirit and essential conflicts of Russian society in the last century—indeed grapples with many of man's fundamental questions about existence—its validity and profundity stem from the narrative art of Tolstoy. Technique and form are inseparable from theme and world-view. On this view, a significant novel is both an autonomous creation and, by virtue of its autonomy, a reflection of the author's striving to apprehend the dilemmas of his time and place.

It must be mentioned that working with contemporary fiction affords a number of advantages which outweigh the problems usually cited: unpredictably shifting sands of critical standards, public taste, and authors' fads of the moment. In point of fact, the critic is free to hypothesize relatively unencumbered by debts to prior generations of masterful investigators. Being a contemporary of the authors, he is able to gauge from firsthand experience their interpretation of the world around them. He is even able to question them about their own personal backgrounds, goals and attitudes, as is the case in the present study. I acknowledge gratefully the time which Juan Rulfo, Carlos Fuentes, Sergio Galindo, Juan José Arreola, Rosario Castellanos, Vicente Leñero, and Elena Garro so generously made available to me in the summer of 1965. From them, and from Emmanuel Carballo and John S. Brushwood I have learned much.

The recent novel in Mexico has been a rich and dynamic body of literature. Its seriousness of purpose and its artistic creativity merit a corresponding sense of responsibility in those who undertake the necessary task of literary evaluation. With the hope that the study which follows represents a contribution toward fulfilling that responsibility, it is dedicated to Agustín Yáñez, Juan Rulfo, and Carlos Fuentes.

AFTER
THE
STORM

1

BECOMING MASTERS IN THEIR OWN HOUSE

THE NINETEENTH CENTURY, which included Mexico's first seventy-five years of independence from Spanish rule, failed to produce a significant novel. The newborn republic suffered chaos in its first decades, characterized by recurring crises, partial dismemberment by the United States, and a brief monarchical dictatorship imposed by France. The liberal constitution of 1857, won with great difficulty by the Juárez reform movement, was reinstituted in 1867, when French troops had been driven from the country. But it was fated to serve the needs of a new dictator, Porfirio Díaz. In the name of liberalism and positivism, and the official motto, "Order and Progress," the Díaz régime maintained itself in power from 1876 until the Revolution of 1910. It was a bitter and strife-torn century, and no incipient novelists were capable of rising above it to join the august ranks of Stendhal, Balzac, Tolstoy, Dostoyevsky, Galdós, and Melville.

Could this have happened in a fledgling nation like Mexico, largely isolated from Western culture and from the industrial revolution? Since history alone cannot explain with precision the emergence of genius, it might indeed have occurred. The fact is that a succession of writers—Lizardi, Altamirano, Rabasa, López Portillo y Rojas—established a tradition, that of the realist novel. But their works are largely unread today, holding attraction almost exclusively for literary historians.

In general, as Samuel Ramos has indicated in his pioneering study on the psychology of the Mexican,[1] the nineteenth century was one of cultural imitation, of allegiance to imported values, and the model was primarily France. His statement can also be applied to the naturalist novels of Federico Gamboa, around the turn of the century.

An important element in the artistic climate prior to and even during the Revolution is the presence of the modernist poets, who earned significant prestige. Unlike the novelists, they were part of a broader movement linked to other Spanish American countries. A further distinction is that the poets could see themselves as following a poetic tradition which had achieved excellence as early as the seventeenth century, in the sonnets of Sor Juana Inés de la Cruz. As a group they were notable for their insistence on the uniqueness of art and its accessibility to only the cultured minority. Manuel Gutiérrez Nájera, Amado Nervo, and others, while fusing a new movement which successfully innovated in poetic forms, minimized the relationship of literature to social and historical context. The critical comment of Frank Dauster sums up an attitude of this movement: "The great sin of Mexican modernism is its lack of sincerity, the abuse of ingeniousness which is excessively evident. Even in the poetry of the best, it is hard to accept that alluring tone of *preciosité*, overly intimate and far too refined."[2]

Modernism was a genuine literary high point of the pre-Revolutionary era. But in its borrowings from French Parnassianism and French Symbolism, its concern only for an élite, its focus on the subjective sensibilities of the poet, and its esthetic of the exquisite, it was far removed from the realities of the day. Subsequently some of the constructive tenents of modernism were reformulated by the Ateneo de la Juventud (Atheneum of Youth), a gathering, on the eve of the Revolution, of young anti-Porfirian intellectuals dedicated to strengthening Mexican ties with the classic European traditions in art and philosophy. A later manifestation was the poetry of the "Contemporáneos" group of the 1920's, with its vanguardist concern for image and form, and its ontological, often metaphysical themes.

The major literary antecedents of the novel of the Revolution, then, were an imitative, discursive novel of realism, following European guidelines, and a more original poetic movement, which stressed the exclusive, estheticist aspects of creative literature. The novel of the Revolution was to assert itself in sharp distinction from both sets of literary values.

As in the case of poetry, the trajectory of Mexican art varies significantly from that of the novel. Pre-Hispanic art has been visibly present throughout the centuries, as has a vigorous popular art tradition carried on by Indian and *mestizo* artists. The pinnacle of creative expression during three centuries of Spanish colonial rule was baroque church art and architecture, which often bear the distinguishing imprint of the Indian artesan. The nineteenth century saw the founding of the Academy of San Carlos, which was important to the institutionalizing of a Mexican tradition, although it added little of originality to world art. The Mexican mural movement, partly a reaction against this academic tradition, was catalyzed by the Revolution and achieved monumental success in Mexico and the major art centers of the world. Taking its themes from the immediate past of revolutionary struggle and suffering, as well as from the drama of Mexican history from pre-Hispanic times to the present, the school of Rivera, Orozco and Siqueiros evolved techniques and forms which incorporated both indigenous and European traditions. Achieving a high point in Mexican art, they arrived at universality by masterful interpretation of the essence of the national spirit.

By the 1950's, a new generation of artists, still following the patterns of the muralists, failed to find a new synthesis of form and theme adequate to a changed post-Revolutionary Mexico, and fell into the trap of imitation. The reaction against a now institutionalized and less dynamic mural movement has been led by José Luis Cuevas who, in order to challenge the old excellence, has had to produce an original new art, stressing detailed refinements of technique and a more direct, personal approach to universal themes.

The novel of the Revolution, coinciding chronologically with the rise of the mural movement, runs a different course. Evaluation requires a clarification of literary terms.

Some important Mexican critics, Antonio Castro Leal for one, have adopted criteria which contain this movement within narrow boundaries. Castro Leal states, in his introduction to the two-volume Aguilar collection of twenty-one complete novels: "By novel of the Mexican Revolution we understand the aggregate of narrative works, in length greater than a simple extended short story, which take their inspiration from the military and popular actions—as well as the political and social changes—which resulted from the diverse movements (peaceful and violent) of the Revolution, which begins with the Madero rebellion . . . of 1910, and whose military phase can be considered to end with the death of Venustiano Carranza . . . in 1920."[3]

In this chapter, a more extended meaning will be used, to take into account not only the sociopolitical nature of the subject matter, but literary standards as well. Seeing the Revolution in its broadest terms supplies a logic for the scope of the Mexican novel from 1915-1947. The common spiritual denominator for this entire period of narrative fiction is a literary nationalism which, in the long run, proves to be of enormous positive value in the evolution of the modern Mexican novel.

The Revolution in its fullest sense is a thirty-year phenomenon, comprising three basic phases, each of which is reflected in Mexican prose fiction. The essence of this body of literature can not be grasped through a descriptive cataloguing of its works, but requires a close examination of the three major novels which exemplify each of these phases.

The first decade, 1910 to 1920, began with the violent overthrow of the Díaz dictatorship. This was followed by the tragic internecine warfare between rival Revolutionary generals—Villa, Carranza, Obregón, and Zapata—a phase characterized by the struggles inherent in the genesis of a new order. Imbued with a sense of destruction, tragedy, and human limitations, Mariano Azuela's *The Underdogs (Los de abajo)*, written in 1915, captures the immediacies of armed struggle. It truly reflects the holocaust.

The interim period from 1920 to 1934 was dominated by Presidents Obregón and Calles. Counterrevolutions were repulsed, national power was consolidated, and the first fruits of revolutionary reform were realized: initial land distribution, popular education, formation of trade unions. *Shadow of the Tyrant (La sombre del caudillo)*, by Martín Luis Guzmán (1929), treats the personal contradictions attendant upon the accumulation and organization of power during this consolidating period. As in Azuela's novel, Guzmán's assessment, as he explores the labyrinth of political intrigue, is critical.

The final stage, 1934 to 1940, corresponding to the presidential term of Lázaro Cárdenas, was marked by sweeping and radical reforms in all aspects of Mexican life. In addition to vast land distribution and a dynamic rural education program, Cárdenas sponsored the first concentrated campaign to improve the lot of the Indian. National unity reached its highest peak in 1938, when all segments of society rallied to support the government expropriation of foreign oil holdings. In literature, Mauricio Magdaleno's *Sunburst (El resplandor)*, of 1937 vintage, constitutes an example of the climate of reform prevailing then, and of the new consciousness of the Indian as the bedrock of national identity.

The Underdogs (Los de abajo)

SINCE ITS BELATED RECOGNITION in 1924, *The Underdogs (Los de abajo)* has become widely accepted as a classic of twentieth-century Mexican letters.[4] It is the first major novel of the Revolution, and remains to this day its most important. Translated into countless foreign editions, for four decades it has supplied the world's readers with their basic image of the Mexican novel. While this image is no longer valid, Azuela still is the most widely read author of the revolutionary period, both in Mexico and abroad.

Perhaps because the novel first appeared in serial form in a newspaper, and because its first complete edition bore the subtitle, "Sketches and Scenes of the Mexican Revolution," critics have tended to stress its episodic quality. Professor Luis Leal, who has written the most authoritative study on Azuela, states: ". . . although the episodes are presented without any order, the personality of Demetrio imparts unity to them: the action begins with the victory of Demetrio over federal troops in the canyon of Juchipila and ends with his death in the same place. The organization of the material, nevertheless, does not follow a premeditated plan. The novel, like the Revolution itself and its men, has no plan at all."[5]

On the contrary, the episodes which comprise the sequence of events are clearly linked together by an overall sense of novelistic structure. The plot, developing with a relentless pace which is one of the novel's distinctive features, traces, on one level, the stark drama of the rise and fall of Demetrio Macías. On a second level, linked to the first by the constant use of symbolic references, the novel sketches the trajectory of the Mexican Revolution, in the anguished interpretation of Mariano Azuela. As in many a more modern novel, the reader is called upon to participate: he must fill out each individual scene, amplifying the suggestive details supplied by the author; he must create a mental image of events between chapters which illuminate only decisive or typical moments in Demetrio's fortunes; finally, if the author's narrative techniques have successfully infused symbolic meaning into his story, the reader must meditate upon its ultimate meaning, its implications concerning the Revolution and Mexican society—for *The Underdogs* is above all a social novel. But the literary clues are present and the reader's path is clearly marked—at times too clearly.

Organic unity of plot is one means by which Azuela elaborates theme. The very first pages supply a traditional "inciting incident": the burning of Demetrio's house by the *federales*, which propels him inexorably into the role of outsider, rebel, and enemy of the existing order. Part I follows the formation of Demetrio's ragged outlaw band, their initial guerrilla-style victory over federal troops, and their regrouping in the shelter of a sympathetic *rancho* community. Luis Cervantes, middle-class opportunist and pseudo-intellectual, joins the group at this stage. His is a dual role. On the one hand, he provides ironic contrast between the elemental ignorance of Demetrio and the principles and ideals embodied in the slogans of the Revolution. On the other, he is the vehicle by which the band is absorbed into the mainstream of the Revolution. This section ends with the heroic participation of Demetrio, now a colonel, in the taking of Zacatecas.

The second section traces Demetrio's fortunes from the heady days of victory, followed by scenes of debauchery, looting and squandering of new-found power, through the Revolution's detour into factionalism. In contrast with the dynamic ascent to power of the first part, the second terminates with the outbreak of armed hostilities between Villa and Carranza forces, after Demetrio's blind pledge of fealty to a "villista" faction. Part III swiftly brings the novel to its end. Demetrio, now a general, leads his men in the vagaries of Villa's futile struggle for supreme control over the Revolution. In an atmosphere of growing doubts and increasing cruelty and slaughter, defeat impends. Demetrio's brief and bitter reunion with his wife and child is followed by his death, the culminating irony of *The Underdogs:* he dies in an ambush in the same canyon of Juchipila from which he had begun his meteoric career.

From this circular plot structure emerges the central theme: the cyclical nature of existence. Revolutions and heroism notwithstanding, the destiny of man—in Mexico at least—is a tragic return to the point from which he started.

Further reinforcing the sense of organized plot structure is the skillful handling of various subplots. These perform the internal function of interrelating the three sections, and play the thematic role of strengthening the central irony around which the novel is constructed. Thus, paralleling the burning of Demetrio's house in Part I is his revenge in Part II, as he puts to the torch the home of the *cacique* who had sent the federal troops—a revenge made more dramatic and cathartic by Demetrio's refusal to allow the home to be looted before its destruction. The career of Luis Cervantes stands in suggestive contrast to that of Demetrio. In Part I, Cervantes cleverly uses revolutionary slogans to win himself a place in the Macías band, which he judges to be on the winning side. In Part II, as Demetrio's secretary, he maintains a sharp eye for loot and personal gain. At the novel's end, having fled before imminent disaster, he is found in Texas, a small businessman with petty ambitions. Other examples, such as the secondary characters Camila and Margarito, have the same subordinate, contrastive function. These are the elements from which Azuela has woven a finished literary fabric, with all plot ends conscientiously tied together. His tight system of internal patterns adds expressiveness to the closed case which the author develops against the idealistic and progressive possibilities of the Revolution.

Elliptical style is also an essential technique in *The Underdogs,* a method markedly unlike the lengthy discursive novels of Federico Gamboa, the immediate predessor of Azuela. Brushstroke descriptions and dialogue compressed to

minimum length with maximum suggestivity, frequently ful-
fill a number of purposes. Short glimpses of landscape not
only serve to set the scene, but underline the antithesis between the majestic serenity of nature and the sordid bestial-
ity of man. At other moments, one-sentence references to
natural phenomena emphasize the mood of a scene or en-
large it with symbolic meaning. Dialogue, always terse, au-
thenticates the various types of personality by the directness
and peculiar flavor of peasant language. A frequent device
is half-dialogue, presenting the speech of one person only,
with the other half of the conversation omitted because it can
be understood by implication. The effect of this stylistic
economy is to approximate the headlong pace of the Revolution, constantly in motion, constantly cutting off meditation
or expression in favor of action and movement.

The amplification of meaning beyond the immediacies
of plot enables Azuela, at least in part, to transcend the limitations of a purely anecdotal story. A variety of techniques
combine to add this dimension. Language, for example, establishes the dehumanization which characterizes not only
the particular lives of Demetrio and his men, but the entire
atmosphere of the Revolution. The use of animal imagery is
one means used to convey the brutality to which man is reduced. After the battle of Zacatecas: "The slope . . . was
covered with corpses, with hair enmeshed, clothing stained
with earth and blood, and in that heaping of warm cadavers,
ragged women scurried about like rapacious coyotes, searching and stripping."[6] At the first encounter between Demetrio
and La Pintada, female camp-follower: "Demetrio, without
understanding, lifted his glance toward her. They stared at
each other face to face like two strange dogs smelling one
another with suspicion." Or the brief but telling description
of the savagery of a cockfight, in which the terms of the com-

parison between man and animal are reversed: "The fight, extremely short, was of a ferocity that was almost human."

Metaphoric symbolism, by which actions or events are explicitly or implicitly infused with extended significance, is introduced at a number of crucial points in the novel. As the historic battle of Zacatecas comes to an end, Solís and Cervantes sit on a hill commenting and observing. Both have avoided combat, Solís out of cynical disillusionment, and Cervantes because of fear. The final thoughts of Solís, just before a sniper's bullet reaches him, prefigure the novel's course: "His smile wandered, following the spirals of smoke from the rifles and the dust from each caved-in house and each roof that collapsed. And he thought he discovered a symbol of the revolution in those clouds of smoke and those clouds of dust that fraternally climbed, embraced each other, blurred together and were obliterated into nothing."

A highly expressive metaphoric action, which has been cited by many critics, occurs in the final stages of the novel, when Demetrio has a momentary reunion with his wife. Weeping, she begs him to return home, asking why he must still fight. Demetrio picks up a stone and throws it down the steep canyon slope. His answer: "See that stone, how it doesn't stop . . ."

But the literary value of *The Underdogs* is circumscribed by the limitations of the period, which tended to subject the author to the extreme pressures and drama of the situation around him. His attention was necessarily focused upon the immediate, and he strove for the authenticity of firsthand experience, finding little time for meditation, subtlety, or profundity.

The emphasis on dramatic and violent elements of the Revolution is confined to their external aspects, that is to the camera's-eye view of a keen observer. The result is superficial, without the internal tension and conflict that in human terms accompany crisis. True, the thesis of Azuela is that man is dehumanized by the cosmic force of the Revolution, which at one moment he likens to a hurricane. Nonetheless, this thesis would be more meaningfully developed through detailing the complexities of character. The reader never apprehends the personal, individual makeup of the central characters, who remain mere types. They are described in terms of their reactions to environmental forces, and in each case follow a consistent pattern, never revealing hesitations or contradictions. Another reason for the lack of complex personalities is that the author fails to supply any real pasts for his characters, whether by flashback, remembrances or other means. Particular actions of Demetrio or Luis, therefore, tend to be accepted as typical, since there is no individual set of causal circumstances which explains them.

A similar lack of causality characterizes the development of plot, which is the essential element in the novel's structure. The plot is shaped by history, by the author's interpretation of a brief but decisive period of the Revolution. But the sense of history is shallow and limits itself to the present. Despite his literary talent in extending meaning, Azuela never links the Mexican present to the past, and the drama of the moment thus lacks any meaningful historical perspective. What were the basic causes of the Revolution? The Revolution was more than the confluence of a series of isolated peasant rebellions against brutal landowners, and the opportunism of a tiny minority of slogan-mongers. Thus, the larger literary interpretation for which Azuela was striving is limited to the human tragedy of a single year, 1914-1915. It never achieves a sweeping view, for the author, like his characters, was overwhelmed by immediate events.

Finally, despite its highly developed artistic qualities, *The Underdogs* suffers from an unevenness in technique. There are occasional repetitions of images, which tend to stand out in such a concise work. "The moon invaded the mountain with blurred shadows," ". . . blurred and disturbing shadows began to invade the mountain." But there are also lapses into stylistic commonplace: "Demetrio squeezed Camila amorously around the waist, and who knows what words he whispered in her ear." And incidents which depend on highly improbable coincidence constitute a decided weakness in a novel whose flavor depends on verisimilitude. Such an incident is the "chance" meeting of Solís and Cervantes on the battlefield at Zacatecas.

At a few points in the novel, the narrative point of view is inconsistent, especially when the removed, impartial narrator abandons his distance and enters the novel to make a direct comment, a frequent convention in nineteenth-century Mexican fiction. An example occurs shortly after Cervantes' arrival among Demetrio's men, when the narrator exclaims to the reader his surprise at their harsh reception: "But see how today, hardly had he arrived among his comrades when they, instead of receiving him with open arms, shut him up in a hogsty!"

WORLD VIEW

While novelistic shortcomings limit the profundity of Azuela's analysis of dilemmas of the Mexican Revolution, *The Underdogs* nevertheless projects a coherent set of concepts which comprise the author's world view.

The Revolution, for Azuela, is hardly a monumental success in achieving social reforms. Its initial character is that of a revolt against Porfirian injustices. Its leaders are motivated by a narrow range of personal goals—a desire for power among the middle class elements, and the avaricious possession of women, horses, and loot, by the exploited peasants who provide the manpower. Fueled by these aspirations, as well as by the drive for revenge, the Revolution soon acquires an independent and fascinating momentum of its own, sweeping along with it the destinies of men and women who come in its path. In reality, its stated goals of land, liberty, and justice are marginal. In the long run, its leaders and its followers, lacking in morality, will reap the anguish that they have sown with their excesses of violence, cruelty, and greed.

As interpreted by Azuela, the Mexican temperament is imperfect, blemished in its primitive nature by an inability to subordinate elemental passions. Solís, the disillusioned idealist, whose voice is closest to that of his author-creator, is asked to explain the circumstances which caused his bitter disenchantment: "Circumstances? . . . Little things, insignificant things. Facial expressions no one notices; the momentary gleam of an eye or curl of a lip; the fleeting meaning of a phrase that is lost. But circumstances, grimaces and expressions, taken together in their logical meaning, compose the frightful and grotesque mask of our race. . . . an unredeemed race!" In the subsequent battle scene, Solís expresses the depth of his pessimism: ". . . the psychology of our race, condensed into two words: rob, kill!"

In dramatic counterpoint to Azuela's judgment of barbarism, his characters display a number of positive qualities under pressure. The fact that they are not redeeming virtues makes them all the more tragic. Demetrio and his men are capable of primitive solidarity and loyalty, of devotion to their leaders, of epic feats of heroism under fire, and of a moving expressiveness in their language and folk songs. Yet they are doomed because their lives and their actions do not respond to even an elemental system of ethical and moral values. For Azuela, the sins of society which provoked the Revolution are perpetuated by the new régime as it rises to power. The Mexican, fallen from grace, continues in his unredeemed state.

In his focus on the representative Mexican rather than on individualized characters, Azuela conveys his view that the individual is a helpless creature prey to the omnipotence of social forces. Noting this aspect of *The Underdogs,* Enrique Anderson Imbert has stated: "Azuela's objectivity is naturalistic in nature: circumstances are determinant; man, without liberty, without goals, is like an animal."[7] Two corollaries can be added. First, it is man's own lack of morality which prevents him from rising above the deterministic forces controlling his destiny. In this connection, it is significant that religious values and consciousness are conspicuously absent in the novel. Secondly, in Azuela's interpretation, the thrust of the Revolution is uninfluenced by meaningful ideas or intellectual leadership, direct or indirect. The novel has distinct anti-intellectual implications in its total omission of the ideological ferment which middle-class elements traditionally contribute to revolutionary situations. On the contrary, the three figures with possible intellectual stature are a corrupt opportunist, a bitterly disillusioned idealist, and a mad poet.

The intense human drama of *The Underdogs,* its taut literary construction, and its symbolic eloquence are characteristics which distinguish it from any prior novel. Despite his novel's limitations in form and thematic depth, Azuela is the first significant Mexican author of the present century.

Shadow of the Tyrant (La sombra del caudillo)

Critics usually contrast Mariano Azuela and Martín Luis Guzmán. The unadorned and direct prose of the former is contraposed against the richer, more elaborate language of Guzmán. Moreover, there is no question but that *Shadow of the Tyrant*[8] is enhanced by expressive imagery, by descriptive detail, and by the rounded development of individual scenes. It moves more slowly than *The Underdogs,* portraying a world which is quite distinct—the tense political circles in which leaders of the Revolution move as they vie for power in the late 1920's. The antithesis of the novel of the anonymous masses, this *roman à clef* concentrates exclusively on a few political chieftains in Mexico City, who hold in their hands the destiny of the Revolution itself. In pace and social setting, as well as style, the two novels are at variance.

While these are valid aspects for contrast, more significant are the qualities in common which place the two works in the same genre. Like Azuela's novel, *Shadow of the Tyrant* has a traditional form, since it narrates a dramatic series of circumstances quite close to historical events. The unnamed *caudillo* whose presence pervades the novel, and whose decisions determine its outcome, obviously corresponds to General Plutarco Elías Calles, President of Mexico from 1924 to 1928. On the other hand, the novel's protagonist, General Ignacio Aguirre, is not an identifiable personage. His fictional experiences suggest, but do not record, those of several actual figures from the Calles period. This literary method, traditional in the historical novel, was also used by Azuela, whose fictional Demetrio Macías exists in the shadow of the historical Pancho Villa.

Both novels also depend upon linear plot for their effectiveness. The Guzmán work centers on the political fortunes of Ignacio Aguirre, Minister of War during the presidency of the *caudillo*. Dynamic and ambitious, he has arrived at this position by virtue of military service during the years of revolutionary warfare—service under the favor and protection of the man who rose to the presidency. Changing political trends, personal aspirations, and conflicts of interest with his superior gradually push Aguirre into the camp of the oppositionists. The latter, motivated by the exigencies of their mutual interests, persuade him to enter the presidential race in opposition to the general whom the *caudillo* has handpicked as his political successor.

As in the Azuela novel, the narrative sequence traces the flow of events on two levels—in this case, the political and the personal. There are scenes which, in subtle detail, follow the process by which support for a candidate is marshalled from a manipulated political convention. Descriptive passages bring to life the dramatic confrontation of the two political factions in a packed Chamber of Deputies, where violence is uncontainable as paid political claques inhabit and overflow the galleries. Interspersed between such scenes are chapters which fill in the personal dimensions of the protagonist—his various amours, his attempts to placate the *caudillo*, his loyalty to two close friends who represent the poles of his own personality—one is an idealistic opposition deputy, the other a corrupt dealer in political influence.

The denouement, after a suspenseful buildup of sordid and occasionally violent political maneuvers and counter-

measures on both sides, finds the Aguirre group outflanked.
Their only resort is the threat of an armed uprising, harking
back to the prior decade of the Revolution and the military
struggle for supremacy. This revolt is broken up by the skillful application of presidential power, and the Aguirre group,
betrayed by a former ally, is taken prisoner. Ruthless assas-
sination on a lonely road is their ultimate fate.

Like *The Underdogs, Shadow of the Tyrant* captures
the sordid dimensions of human ambition spurred into competition by a crisis of power within the Revolution. In the
earlier novel, the Villa-Carranza rivalry was the background;
here it is the Calles struggle to retain leadership by hand-
picking a successor. The narrative point of view is similarly
removed and objective. Although not unsympathetic to the
Aguirre alliance, the author nevertheless carefully details
their recourse to the tactics of the tyrant.

The plot of *Shadow of the Tyrant* is limited to the fluc-
tuations of one election campaign, and its setting is the warfare of politics rather than the battlefield. But the same cor-
relation between the fortunes of the protagonist and those of
the Revolution, as in *The Underdogs,* enlarges the novel's
reference. In this case, enlargement stems not from the implications of literary symbols, but from a direct focus on the
leaders of the Revolution which examines their personalities,
motivations, and policies.

Narrative detachment sharpens Guzmán's representa-
tion of the corruption which undermines both sides and in-
hibits revolutionary progress. Vivid, semiautonomous scenes,
elaborated in a fresh and luminous style, recall some of the
same motifs seen in Azuela. Opportunism, hypocrisy, cynicism, sexual immorality, cruelty, and violence are still the
underlying norms of conduct, although their expression in

Guzmán's novel acquires forms which characterize the middle stage of the Revolution.

A scene displaying most of these norms occurs when Aguirre appeals to the sense of justice of the Machiavellian *caudillo*. He brings to the latter written proof that Jiménez, the presidential favorite, ordered the kidnapping and torture of Aguirre's close friend, a proponent of Aguirre's presidential candidacy. Here the politician cynically and incontrovertibly parries every attempt by Aguirre to introduce ethical principles.

The Caudillo took the three sheets of paper handed to him by his minister, read them very slowly, kept them and then said with the poise of his best moments—a poise which generated the strength of his iridescent smile:

"An interesting story, no doubt of it. But I deny the authenticity of the facts. Hilario, as an official and a man, is above such petty trivialities."

"And if I assured you that everything described there is true?"

With this question, Aguirre was striving to block off all possible evasion.

"Well then I would think," replied the President, "that your emotions are blinding you, and I'd recommend that you take it to the courts."

Aguirre, excited, forgot his normal respectful address.

"But I could answer to that, General, that the courts, for a man with the political power of Jiménez, are also petty trivialities!"

"No, Aguirre, you wouldn't answer that way. Because things like that, when I'm governing the country, are not said in my presence."

And the Caudillo had removed his glasses, accentuating above the tone of his gray mustache in disorder, his expression which was at once smiling and overbearing. From his eyes, like a tiger's, emanated flashes, magnificent flashes of color.[9]

As in almost all novels of the Revolution, events in *Shadow of the Tyrant* are recounted in the third person and follow the logic of chronological sequence. Unshaded by subplots or by significant attention to minor characters, the story concentrates on the drama of Ignacio Aguirre. The setting of personal history within an extended political context is essential to the novel's interest, as is the element of suspense created by the interaction of personal and political tensions. Uncomplicated in its structure, traditional in its narrative technique, creative in its use of language, the novel organizes its attention to one central theme: the inevitable corruption attendant upon the achieving and maintaining of political power.

Sharing the weakness of his predecessor, Guzmán fails to probe in depth into the personality of his central character. Viewed from the outside, the interesting and even contradictory behavior of Aguirre affords insufficient help in solving his personality. In the absence of any meaningful set of antecedent experiences or formative influences, he appears a one-dimensional creature of the present. Explanation is lacking as to why he is, on the one hand, brave, likeable, and loyal to friends and, on the other, addicted to women, open to immoral dealings, and a victim of the seductions of power. Apparent contradictions indicate clearly the unexplored possibilities for complexity of motivation and for the internal tensions necessary to define character. Superficially treated, Aguirre does not transcend stereotype.

The novel is similarly limited in historical perspective. A novel which is based upon an interpretation of historical events must take into account the play of forces which makes up the element of causality. There is no suggestion of how the *caudillo* had achieved power or conserved it, beyond the view of his tactics in dealing with subordinates on a personal level. We know nothing of what is going on beneath the surface of a power struggle or what has gone on before. Whereas in Azuela's work we were aware only of masses in motion without leadership, here we see the Revolution only through the machinations of a handful of leaders. The resulting simplistic view of history which underlies the novel sharply limits its reference to the specific set of circumstances which obviously embittered Martín Luis Guzmán.

WORLD VIEW

The overall view of man and Mexico in *Shadow of the Tyrant* essentially resembles that of *The Underdogs*, particularly in its attitude of bitterness and cynicism in evaluating the status of the Revolution. In Guzmán's interpretation from the vantage point of 1929, it is an arena in which corrupt politicians with revolutionary reputations contend ruthlessly for power. The concepts of popular participation, of social change, of democratic ideals—these play no role in his pessimistic view of a Mexico in the shadow of a despot. For the *caudillo*, the Revolution has served only the double function of a training ground in tactics and a ladder to power.

In the fictional world which Guzmán fashioned from Mexico as he saw and judged it, intellectual values exert minimal influence. In the few scenes in which peasants and

Indians appear, they are docile, uncomprehending foils for the maneuvers of their superiors. The middle classes, who might possibly have provided leadership and a sense of values for the Revolution, are depicted in the novel as they stand scornfully aloof, watching a parade of the poor after the political convention in Toluca. Axaná, the idealist politician, comments bitingly, in words which express the disillusionment of the author: ' "Take a good look," said Axaná to Mijares, "look at the smiles of these 'decent folks.' They're so lacking in any sense of civic responsibility that they don't even realize that they are to blame for Mexican politics being what it is. I don't know which is greater, their stupidity or their faint-heartedness." '

Ideas are never exchanged among the politicians and generals who make up the novel's cast. One vague discussion in which the concept of honor enters is outweighed by innumerable dialogues centering on political tactics. On the only occasion in which ideas are proffered in any sense other than as slogans—a speech by Axaná to the peasants—they prove to be precisely the least effective aspect of his spellbinding oratory: "The ideological structure of his phrases was the waste which fell to the ground; the intuitive, irrational elements—generating enthusiasm and hope—went straight to their hearts. In his speech concepts had no life: words lived as individual entities, with esthetic value, having essential value by the sole virtue of their immediate effect on the soul. . . ."

In the social mode of Aguirre and the *caudillo*, actions and words are at the service of emotions and desires. Just as there is no room for intellectual concepts, moral values are equally absent. Part of Aguirre's tragedy lies in the fact that he is less cynical than the *caudillo,* and has at least some imperfect notions of a code of ethics. But, ultimately, this merely renders him vulnerable. In the end, he realizes the supreme truth contained in the aphorism of one of his political allies: "Mexican politics conjugates only one verb: to ambush." The novel dramatically proves that ruthless power subjugates any code which includes elements of loyalty, conscience, and decency. It projects a view of the Mexican in his Revolution as unable to master reason or morality and, therefore, falling victim to a tyranny which creates new forms for the violence of old.

More concerned than Azuela with the expressiveness of language, Guzmán illuminates the emotions of his characters through impressionistic imagery, and provides poetic background to dramatize individual scenes. A suspenseful novel of the Revolution, *Shadow of the Tyrant* has integrity as a genuine work of literary creation. But it does not achieve the epic starkness, the monumentality, or the tragic depth of *The Underdogs*.

Sunburst (El resplandor)

By 1937 the revolutionary reform program had gained momentum. The chronic instability caused by imminent revolts had decreased, and there had been time to develop a semiofficial ideology. *Sunburst (El resplandor)*,[10] published that year, reflects the intellectual atmosphere of the Cárdenas period, dynamic, *engagé*, and militant.

It is a novel of strong social protest. The Indian is its subject, and the projected readership is the educated middle class of Mexico, largely concentrated in the nation's capital. Unlike Azuela and Guzmán, both of whom wrote from abroad as disillusioned exiles, Mauricio Magdaleno worked at home, at a time when an intellectual might influence the course of events. Preoccupation with the Indian—his ancient culture, tragic history, and current status—was the order of the day. Of the three novels under discussion, Magdaleno's is the only one containing explicitly tendentious criticism, presented with hope of provoking reform.

Like *Shadow of the Tyrant*, the novel is set in the Calles period, but here similarities begin to fade. Although both works level severe criticism at political corruption, the literary substance and techniques of each are vastly different.

A regional, nonurban novel, *Sunburst* focuses on an Otomí Indian community, and it is the community itself which proves to be Magdaleno's protagonist. The work is ambitious in structure and scope, more than twice the length of *The Underdogs* and half again as long as the Guzmán novel. Magdaleno recognized that an effective dramatization of the Indians' plight required treating it as an unending repetition of the same pattern of exploitation, whether at the hands of the Spanish *conquistador* or his *mestizo* heirs. He devoted a full third of his narrative to fictional antecedents of the novel's events. The past, in Magdaleno's terms, has considerable meaning in explaining man's contemporary experience.

The first of three roughly equal sections introduces the miserable Otomí village of San Andrés de la Cal, in its sunscorched setting, just as the priest deserts it. From that point on, the entire section is a series of juxtaposed flashbacks. We first witness the perennial feud with the neighboring Indians of San Felipe, and the killings which caused the priest to abdicate his post in despair. The third-person narration then moves back to earlier days when armed revolutionary bands had moved through the region, some of them recruiting Indians with promises—still unfulfilled—of bread and land. Now the narrative swings as far back in time as it can go—to the Conquest—in order to trace the process by which the Fuentes family gained control of La Brisa, the fertile, cultivated *hacienda* for which nearby San Andrés serves as labor and service pool. The first swaggering Fuentes arrives, bursting with Renaissance ambition and self-confidence, to claim La Brisa and take the Indians of San Andrés in *encomienda*, as his serfs. Subsequent Fuentes generations, less dynamic but more pious and wily, align themselves with the church, which serves their interests both as a pacifier of the Indians and a purveyor of aristocratic prestige. Clearly, this structuring of the past of San Andrés is in accord with the nationalist interpretations of history then current.

The scene changes to the Díaz era, when Gonzalo Fuentes maintained an iron grip on La Brisa and San Andrés in the name of Porfirian "Order and Progress." The onslaught of the Revolution in 1910 draws his peon Olegario away from La Brisa, sweeping him into a series of chaotic experiences recounted in scenes which recall the early fiction of the Revolution. Olegario finally returns to die in San Andrés, leaving with the village elders a *mestizo* child, Saturnino. A few years later, a paternal governor passing through San Andrés chooses this child to be educated in the state capital of Pachuca.

This first part, slow-moving and ponderous, extends the chronological sequence by a series of flashbacks. Its sluggishness, however, stems not from the flashbacks themselves or from their nontemporal order, but from an excess of sentimental verbiage and repetitive description. Nonetheless, this initial section introduces all important characters, sketches the tragic history of San Andrés, traces continued Fuentes hegemony, and utilizes the flavor of revolutionary turmoil to show the origin of Saturnino. At the same time, it establishes the tragic tone of Indian suffering which suffuses the entire novel.

The second part, now in the present of the Calles period, follows strict chronological order. It builds gradually to a climax, based on the conflicts created when Saturnino returns to San Andrés. Now a politician, married to the sole surviving member of the Fuentes family, he is a candidate for state governor and needs the Indians' support. His promises overcome their doubts and despair, firing up new hopes as they dream of sharing in the bounty of La Brisa. They ardently enlist, sending mass delegations to support Saturnino, while he secretly formulates plans to restore the *hacienda* razed during the Revolution, using Indian labor to create a personal neo-Porfirian fief. This second part, pointing up an inevitable clash of interests, ends on the triumphant crest of Saturnino's election.

The third section proceeds to the inevitably tragic ending. The Indians gradually become aware that their labor on La Brisa, supposedly an experimental project, is not in their own interest. The brutal tactics of Saturnino's administrator meet desperate resistance, which culminates in a riot and the administrator's death. Troops pour in to San Andrés to exact reprisal in the form of mass hangings. A bitter peace restored, softer tactics are introduced to harness Indian labor to the continuing task of developing the *hacienda*, including the assignment to the village of an idealistic schoolteacher. But the novel ends with the deepened Indian awareness of misfortunes inexorably repeated. To the horror of the villagers, for whom the parallel is all too obvious, a new child is selected, in a magnanimous gubernatorial gesture, to be educated in the state capital.

Sunburst generates a powerful emotional impact. Its fundamental theme stands out, for the author has shaped it in no uncertain terms: the calamitous fate of the Indian, exploited monotonously and for the same fundamental economic reasons by each succeeding generation across four centuries of Mexican history. The Revolution, of course, merely gives new form to the same set of relationships. An important corollary of this central theme is the hopeless choice faced by the Indian between adhering to his own basically indigenous culture, which is presented as completely inadequate, or coming to terms with modern capitalist society, which uses him as a pawn. A considerable measure of the novel's impact derives from the historical dimension, deepening the immediate conflicts dramatized in the plot by explaining their roots in the past, and making more meaningful the profound bitterness of the Indians.

But the thematic development of a novel is inseparable from its style, and the work bends under the weight of highly emotional imagery. "Tropical" is the term employed by José Luis Martínez to describe Magdaleno's use of language.[11] Descriptions are frequently florid and excessively adjectival. Charged with the passions of the author, they exclude the possibility of reader participation. The following paragraphs describe the Indians' desolation when the priest abandons them:

> In remote yesterdays, when the flattening weight of the whites had rolled in upon them, and through years as uncounted as the stars in the skies of San Andrés, they learned that rebellion was futile. Their eyes were drained of tears, their voices turned meek and confi-

dential. There was an indifference in them now, like ashes on a log burned to embers. Life burst from the womb with no audible spasm of torment. Death was an incident that broke in on young and old without interrupting a task or ebbing the flow of energy. Energy, in this land of the Otomí Indians, had become a concentrated vitality, monstrously paralleling the minerals and the cactus.

Fifty years, a hundred years, were nothing—a moment of existence on the plateau. Over there, on the other side of the hill, said the Indian: and a traveler might go on for days and still not arrive. Over the hill, in twenty years, all the same thing, and the voices reproduced the sameness of the landscape which went on and on endlessly, strange to all notion of time and space. Twenty years . . . eighty years . . . a lifetime, after all, ninety or a hundred, lived, what is the difference for such as cannot dwell on the nervous pulleys of consciousness, for whom birth and death are simply two extremes of a dreadful fate? The rock, the knotty cactus, the mesquite do not complain. Why should the Otomí? He knows this much, that his death will make less difference than that of the ox or the mule that means the livelihood of the family.

Silent, they watched the vehicle disappear in the distance. So the priest was gone. God had left them, as Don Melquiades had said. So, they would get used to doing without him, too.[12]

Such examples indicate a number of weaknesses beyond a penchant for stylistic verbosity. The flavor of discursive essay stands out, with the author presenting his views on Indian psychology in terms of experiences not connected with the novel. These ideas, couched in language aimed at the reader's sentiments, are essentially a form of address from the author directly to the reader, complete with rhetorical questions ("Why should the Otomí?"). In the first section of the novel, the reader does participate somewhat, ordering the flashbacks and filling in between them to form a coherent appreciation of their import. In the latter parts, however, the reader sits back passively to receive an insistent flow of overpowering prose which pushes plot to the brink of melodrama.

Exceptions to this pattern are two occasions in which hallucinatory dream sequences are introduced in an attempt to approximate the elements making up the Indian view of reality. A unique passage is the stream-of-consciousness monologue of Bonifacio, the Indian elder, in the moments before his death by hanging. Unfortunately, these are isolated examples in the body of the narrative.

Like his predecessors, Magdaleno found that the drama of events and their circumstances outweighed the importance of the individual. His characters are simplified and typical. By and large, the Indians, particularly the elders, are sympathetic, kindly, and stoically suffering. When they become violent and destructive, the context makes clear the inevitability of their provocation. *Mestizo* characters, from Saturnino to the village storekeeper, are greedy, hypocritical exploiters, with but slight variations, and Magdaleno's style reinforces this simplification. Descriptive passages weighted with evaluative adjectives stress the moral dignity of the Indians by contrasting them with their filthy surroundings, and underline repeatedly the shrewd duplicity of Saturnino. A few personalities, such as the opportunistic political lieutenants, are so sketchy and so extreme as to be mere caricatures. The one exception, the idealistic school-teacher who appears late in the novel when tragedy has taken definitive shape, is condemned to futility.

If the village of San Andrés is seen as the novel's protagonist, it too emerges as a typified rather than an individualized character. Complexities, tensions, and variations in village life are absent. The past and present of San Andrés is a monotonous fabric, whose texture is determined almost completely by its economic and social subservience to the masters of La Brisa.

World View

Despite a critical attitude toward society, the world view of *Sunburst* is merely that of a more advanced stage of the Revolution. In the first place, it expresses the *indigenismo* which characterized Mexican thought in the 1930's. Its outspoken sympathy for the Indians is reinforced by a black-and-white interpretation of Mexican history which assigns moral guilt to the proponents of Hispanic-Catholic traditions. Underlying this interpretation is the deterministic view that responsibility can be traced to the greed of the exploiters. By implication, genuine land reform and the elimination of political corruption would absolve the emerging Revolution from further guilt.

While on the one hand the novel decries the despoilment of the innocent Indian by iniquitous heirs of Western civilization, on the other hand its view of the Indian is paternalistic. For paternalism was an ingredient of *indigenismo* as interpreted by many Mexican intellectuals of Magdaleno's period. The Indian is portrayed as the prisoner of a culture whose superstitions keep him in ignorance and provide only the inadequate armor of stoicism and a fatalistic acceptance of foreknown suffering. Indian culture is presented from the viewpoint of a non-Indian narrator, who catalogues totemic beliefs, a religion suffused with paganism, and a reliance upon folk medicine, then considers these useless in a Western society. There are few examples of sensitivity to the role of such beliefs and practices within an Indian world view.

On the contrary, the author fails to comprehend that in order to survive and maintain themselves over the centuries, the Otomís of San Andrés must have been able to draw sustenance from their acculturated, syncretic, semi-Christianized set of values. Similarly, Magdaleno affirms in the first chapter that the Indian has a unique conception of time. Yet the novel's retrospection views the Indian in strictly non-Indian temporal terms, tracing his fate across the stages of Mexican history.

While Magdaleno bases *Sunburst* on the contrast of cultures, he develops this contrast using the dominant culture as the norm. The resultant implication is that Indian values are anachronistic, and will contribute little to Mexican national character as the Indian, shedding his old modes, is incorporated into the mainstream.

In a sense, *Sunburst* is less anti-intellectual than the two novels already discussed. It does attempt to examine causality, albeit in the uncomplicated terms of a rather unilateral determinism. However, as in the preceding novels, men of vision are portrayed as complete hypocrites. For Saturnino, ideas are mere slogans, useful as tools of deception; for Pedroza, his pseudo-intellectual subordinate, they constitute necessary embellishments of political power, to be sold for a place in the establishment. The pristine ideals of the schoolteacher, in Magdaleno's interpretation, are unrelated to the hard realities which the novel dramatizes.

The novel's evaluation of the Revolution must be differentiated, however, from the harsh judgments implicit in the earlier novels. *Sunburst* does not pretend to evaluate the immediate moment, but rather the Revolution's course up to a point approximately a decade earlier. Certainly its underlying principles corresponded to those of the latter-day Revolution as proclaimed by the Cárdenas régime, which, at the novel's writing, had just completed the expulsion of Calles from Mexico. More important, the novel represented a challenge to those intellectuals who were formulating new concepts of Mexican nationality. The basic meaning emerging from the dramatic clash of interests in *Sunburst* suggests the continued presence of the Indian as a weight upon the national conscience, and the necessity for the Revolution to take cognizance of him or face resounding failure.

The inability of Magdaleno to separate himself emotionally from his characters, and his insistence on coloring descriptions in order to ensure the proper reaction in the reader are indications of his conception of the novelist as omniscient interpreter of life and the world, set off on a higher level from his audience. Nevertheless, the work represented a significant literary step beyond Azuela and Guzmán. Magdaleno's stressing of historical perspective rendered the interpretation of the present more meaningful in its tragic findings and more powerful in its dramatic impact. The most important *indigenista* novel of the period, it extended the thematic range of the novel of the Revolution. Although without significantly altering the literary character of the novel, Magdaleno did demonstrate a concern for some of the new techniques which, by 1937, had become well known in Europe and the United States: departure from straight chronological sequence, and the attempt to grasp the irrational side of man's nature through dream sequences and stream-of-consciousness narration. Not only in theme, but in its scope, complexity of plot, and its early concern for innovation, *Sunburst* reflects an important stage of growth in the Mexican novel.

Significance of the Movement

Taken as a whole, the novel of the Revolution, from 1915 to 1947, is unified not only by themes emanating from the Revolution, but by similarities among the principal authors in technique and in their views of Mexican man and society. Underlying these congruities are the authors' relationships to the nationalism which, throughout these years, dominated the spirit of Mexican intellectual life.[13]

Just as Mexico was asserting its nationhood through its Revolution, its writers were demonstrating for the first time, to themselves and their readers, that a genuine Mexican novel was possible. Their most obvious recourse was Mexican subject matter treated in a manner which revealed national preoccupation. Central characters were identified by those characteristics which were most typical: popular language and folk songs, as in *The Underdogs*, or folk beliefs, as in *Sunburst*.

The country underwent a process of self-examination, and the novelists had neither time nor concern for their European contemporaries, Proust, Joyce, and Kafka, or for the American "Lost Generation." The giants of the Western world's modern novel had no appreciable literary influence upon these writers, who were immersed in the overwhelming implications of a social upheaval. In fact, those authors of the "Contemporáneos" group (Torres Bodet, Villaurrutia, Owen) who did attempt novels in the mode of Proust and Joyce were criticized sharply as antinational and guilty of "extranjerismo," of having turned their backs upon the reality of Mexico.[14]

Clearly the novel of this period directed its focus neither on problems of ontological scope nor on the perplexities encountered by the individual in society. Rather, it encompassed the range of dilemmas facing Mexico as a nation. It is no accident that themes of love are absent, while social exploitation, corruption of political power, and the omnipresence of violence and death dominate the literature. Similarly, the failure within these works to be concerned with individual psychology is consistent with the focus on man as a member of a national body.

Man is seen as diminished by society—a concept which emerges from the emphasis on plot, the absence of complex characters, and the anti-intellectual tone which predominates. Special characteristics of each novel, such as the rapid pace of *The Underdogs* or the social causality of *Sunburst,* reinforce this concept in particular ways. The common form, stressing anecdote and story development, contributes to this vision of man as unable to control his destiny. Events themselves proceed headlong, dragging characters in their wake. The contingencies of plot are larger than the capacities of protagonists.

Writing as they were from experiences which had transpired during their own adult lives,[15] the authors applied themselves to the most immediate questions at hand, evidencing national consciousness but also conceptual limitations. Thus the absence of introspection, imagination, fantasy, or philosophical musing. Not until Magdaleno, in the

1930's, does even a rudimentary cognizance of historical continuity and causality appear.

If man in his confrontation with society was viewed by these authors through a convex lens, reducing his proportions, his antagonist, by contrast, receives a concave projection. Social forces are so overpowering as to be monolithic. Any dialectical notions of society—political, economic, historical, social—are blurred by simplification. Thus, the novels tend toward finality in their evaluations of man and society. The course of events leaves no room for doubt in novels which close upon themselves, shutting out ambiguity.

Similarly, the use of highly traditional narrative technique in continuation of nineteenth-century patterns constituted a limitation. For the novelists of the Revolution, the realities of the moment were more important than the techniques by which they were presented. With a partial exception in the case of Azuela, they failed to endow their works with thematic depth, not recognizing the relationship between meaning and technique.

The novel of the Revolution was dynamic in capturing the immediacy of a dramatic period in Mexican history. Its originality lies in its sharp definition of many of the problems, anxieties, and modes of expression which distinguished Mexicans from people of other nations in the early twentieth century. That originality contributed to the autochthonous process of self-knowledge over which the Revolution presided. Further, it marked out valid subject matter which the modern novelists would later treat with new perceptions and new literary modes.

At last there was engendered among Mexican writers an important sense of being masters in their own house, of having achieved creative autonomy. The novels were read, commented upon, criticised in leading journals and literary supplements. Novelists came to be figures of genuine stature and social prestige.

Paradoxically, this constructive process of affirmation was achieved through works of literature which were consistently denunciatory, almost uniformly concerned from a moral standpoint with bearing witness to the negation of the principles and program of the Revolution. Even in its formative stages, the twentieth century Mexican novel asserts itself as judge and critic, excoriating the status quo.

AGUSTÍN YÁÑEZ, like Juan Bosch of the Dominican Republic and Rómulo Gallegos of Venezuela, belongs to a vanishing breed in Latin America—the creative writer who plays a decision-making role in the political and social life of his nation. Presently Secretary of Education in the cabinet of President Gustavo Díaz Ordaz, he also served as governor of his native state of Jalisco from 1953 to 1959.

Yáñez has had a rich, varied, and prolific career. He was born in 1904 in Guadalajara, capital of Jalisco. His education there culminated in a law degree in 1929, by which time he had become editor of an important literary journal. Moving on to Mexico City, he spent many years as a Professor at the National University of Mexico, where his interests, in addition to Mexican literature, were in history and esthetics. He has published historical studies on Fray Bartolomé de las Casas, Justo Sierra, and José Joaquín Fernández de Lizardi.

In the domain of narrative fiction he has an extensive personal bibliography which includes some ten volumes of short stories and half a dozen novels. Of these works, only *Al filo del agua* (1947) has been translated into English. Unlike his novels on themes of modern Mexico City, which have met with little success, two recent works set in rural Jalisco—*La tierra pródiga* (1960) and *Las tierras flacas* (1962)—provide examples of Yáñez at his best.

2 | GENESIS OF THE STORM: AGUSTÍN YÁÑEZ

The Edge of the Storm (Al filo del agua)

THE EDGE OF THE STORM is a novel of imminence. Set on "the edge of the storm," during the year and a half leading to and including the first outbreak of 1910, it has the Revolution as a presiding presence.

Yet Yáñez's work is not a historical novel striving to recreate the essential characteristics of a moment in the national past. Rather, it is an intense literary study of the human patterns which make up the contradictory personality of a village in rural Jalisco, illuminated by the violent flashes of lightning of an impending deluge.

Outweighing the extraliterary historical background, the internally generated, rich atmosphere is its prime element of cohesion. The overpowering tension is only partially attributable to the approaching military conflict. The imminence of personal outburst also charges the air.

By comparison with novels of the Revolution which were firmly plotted, *The Edge of the Storm* represents a more ambitious literary effort. It depends upon modern novelistic techniques to create the emotional climate of a village which in physical terms is its setting and in human terms its collective protagonist.

The novel begins, in fact, with an introductory section, whose function is both to set the stage and establish tone, introducing themes rather than elements of the plot. The style of this "Acto preparatorio" draws a somber portrait of the anonymous "village of black-robed women." Static in its vision of a joyless, motionless life dominated by the permanent routine of religious observance; ponderous in its reflection of the town's immutability—heavy stonework, patina-laden door panels, houses topped by crosses of stone and mortar; reiterative in its description of the dry and barren qualities of both landscape and human beings; sonorous in its phrasing, overlaid with the cadence of liturgy, the "Acto preparatorio" creates a series of vivid sense-impressions.

Village of never-ending Lent. Penitential ashes temper the beauties of spring and summer. Constant reminders of the Day of Judgment are poured like Holy Oil into all ears, the Holy Water of repentance is sprinkled on all foreheads; the *Miserere* becomes a constant scourge upon all backs; the precept, 'Remember, O man' is kept constantly before all eyes; in all minds lies the thought of the *Requiem Aeternam*. The Four Horsemen of the Apocalypse, like municipal police, ceaselessly patrol street, house and conscience. 'De profundis' is on every tongue, signs of strict fasting on every brow and cheek.[1]

It is this introduction which later binds together the disparate actions and thoughts of various characters who make up the composite protagonist. The "Acto preparatorio," like a chorus, intones the hidden desires and fears which abound like tangible presences in the night. "Desires and fears are not abstractions," commented one critic, "they are palpitating and palpable members of the community."[2] These vivified symbols permeate the book.

The opening chapter introduces four characters, each in the grip of nighttime contemplation of frustrations. In one brief glimpse after another, personal longings are seen to conflict with the traditions—social, religious, economic, moral—which the community imposes.

The following chapter establishes the narrative pattern of rapid switches from one set of personalities and circumstances to another, always within the overall context of the dominating community and preserving a recognizable time sequence. It introduces in leisurely fashion the parish priest, Don Dionisio Martínez. Sketching his role as the center of village life, the narration encompasses both his observable conduct—his rigorous, Spartan daily routine—and his interior spiritual existence. Here he feels himself directly and personally responsible, as the Lord's shepherd, for guiding each member of his flock through the perils which the impurities of human nature constantly present. The chapter expands its focus from the individual to the collective, passing on to the annual Lenten exercises which dramatize, as they briefly introduce a variety of characters, the themes of guilt and self-chastisement symbolically presented in the "Acto preparatorio."

Succeeding divisions, oscillating between individual and group scenes, present additional characters and gradually establish interrelated subplots. One is the losing struggle of Don Dionisio to keep his flock sheltered against subversive influences from the outside: newspapers reporting political unrest and crimes of violence; seminary students returning home for vacation, bent on pleasure and forced to seek it through clandestine channels; the "northerners," migrant workers repatriated after fieldwork in the United States, bearing the contagion of modern customs and the values of a Protestant society; visitors, such as the attractive widow Victoria, who ignites men's desires.

A key subplot develops the secret love affair between Micaela and the "northerner" Damián. The former, having experienced briefly the heady social whirl of Mexico City, can no longer repress her inner need for relationship with men. The pressures of contained emotions gradually build up until violence inevitably erupts. Damián murders both the flirtatious Micaela and his own father, thereby shaking the town's dwindling sense of security.

A third plot thread is in the influence of Victoria on Gabriel, a melodramatic relationship barely plausible even in the context of the town's atmosphere. Gabriel is the town bell-ringer, the purveyor of routine in a village whose activities are ordered by the tone of ever-present chimes. His artistry with the bells constitutes the only note of creative expression in the village. It is this creativeness which attracts Victoria to the ragged potential musician, and which almost leads to his destruction.

A final subplot involves María, the niece of Don Dionisio, an imaginative girl with no outlet for her fantasies. Her uncle's parental love, compounded by the pain of gradually realizing how ineffectual his upbringing has been, leads to an ironic climax at the novel's end. The storm breaks and revolutionary bands sweep through town. María marches off with them, repudiating her childhood, family, and village in order to search, with the Revolution, for a more constructive future.

But the narrative substance of *The Edge of the Storm* is more than the sum of these and other subplots. Since the protagonist is in essence the village itself, its destiny constitutes the axis of the plot. The personality of the village is rounded out by narrative sequences of a collective nature. The Lenten spiritual exercises, the celebration of Holy Week, the wake for Damián's mother, the activities of such largely anonymous groups as the "northerners," the returning students and the fanatical Daughters of Mary, the popular response to an overnight visit by a band of drunken musicians whose music momentarily sets free long-dormant yearnings for enjoyment and sensual experience—all these give substance to the collective character of the village.

Pieced together, the various narrative components, group and individual, make up the fabric of existence in this isolated community against the background of national crisis. The apparently smooth and massive surface of the village in fact conceals a seething set of repressed desires waiting for expression. At the novel's close, tradition calcified into repression ultimately loses purpose and explodes into a violent upheaval.

NARRATIVE TECHNIQUE AND REALITY

Yáñez has been censured for the ponderous quality of his sequence of events, particularly in the apparently static first half of the novel.[3] But critics have neglected the basic human drama unfolding beneath the surface. Reality for both the village and the inhabitants is comprised of not only objective, observable happenings, but also the subjective world frequently conveyed by interior monologue or expressive poetic symbols as in the "Acto preparatorio." The essence of the novel's structure lies in conflicts and tensions between opposing human drives, personal and social, continually seeking resolution in new forms. This antithetic structure upon which Yáñez has built *The Edge of the Storm* is revealed by a study of its narrative technique.

On a personal level, the key individuals are torn between the contradictory pressures of static and dynamic modes of existence. Life for these characters is an aching duality of unresolved conflicts, which demand solution if personal destruction or tragedy are to be averted. In the lives of María, Don Dionisio, Timoteo, and others, a major thematic conflict is the struggle between the hegemony of death, sin, and guilt as determinants of behavior, and the deep human impulse toward an affirmation of individual personality.

An example of one of several techniques by which Yáñez conveys this inner duality is the interior dialogue of Mercedes, a spinster, as she tosses in bed. A secret letter from a would-be lover touches off a mental clash in which conscience and instinct are represented as separate entities contending for Mercedes' thoughts. The following paragraphs present the beginning and the end of the dialogue:

She put out the light. She was certainly perspiring, but she couldn't get to sleep. She seemed to hear a furtive, persistent step on the sidewalk outside; a breathless panting near her window; low whistles in the street, whistles with a note of desperate pleading.

"It must be nerves," she thought. And her memory answered her with words from the letter: "I have suffered a great deal from your pride, and I may not continue to resist this suffering, which is unjust, because my intentions have been honorable, and I do not deserve your scorn."

"Lies! He's not suffering!"

"But suppose desperation really does make him do something dreadful?"

"I won't be responsible. How could I be?"

. . . . .

"He may be killed, that's what you mean, and you're wishing the death of your fellow man, which is not a Christian thing to do; if it were to happen, remember, he might destroy you first. What then?"

"I won't give in!"

"There's a certain wavering in your determination, as if you were enjoying the danger."

"Maybe."

"Yes, there's a certain pleasure in fighting against the Devil, and you want to make a devil of this man."

"He is the Devil, for me . . ."

"Then I am this man, and I'm already inside you, fighting inside you, gaining ground within you while you think of me . . ."

Other techniques by which Yáñez formulates inner turmoil are secret thoughts, presented conventionally in third

person (María's ruminations and daydreams, hidden from
her uncle); symbolic dreams (Don Dionisio); and brief
thought fragments, presented in quotation marks and in pa-
rentheses, amidst scenes of normal dialogue and description.
(At the wake for Damián's mother these convey his sister's
resentments toward him and their father, while outwardly
she joins in the mourning.)

On the level of the collective protagonist, the poetic
prose of the "Acto preparatorio" initiates the reader into
the tormented inner world of the town, in a Gothic passage
characterized by medieval symbolism:

> On moonlight nights, the spirits of fear and desire es-
> cape in a mad race; one can hear their turbulent flight,
> along the street, over the walls, above the rooftops.
> Straitjackets fling about in the air, fists are clenched,
> fingers twist skirts; they beat against the silence of the
> houses, blindly, like big black birds in flight: birds with
> the wings of vampires, owls or hawks; of doves, too,
> stupid doves who, having just escaped, will soon come
> back submissively to the cage. On moonlight nights, it
> is the spirits of desire which always lead; the fears run
> behind, threatening, urging them to wait, screaming
> harsh imprecations, borne along, with shrill, incompre-
> hensible cries, on the wings of the wind. The spirits of
> desire dart to and fro, from light to shadow, from
> shadow to light. In vain the fears try to follow their
> course. The age old dance goes on till past midnight.
> And in the early hours of the morning, when the bells
> ring in the dawn but the moon is still in the sky, the
> stormy struggle of fears and desires begins again.
> Morning brings victory to the fears, and all day long
> they will be the first to roam around the church pre-

cincts, the streets, the square, while the desires lie concealed in lines etched on faces and brows, hidden under lowered lashes, in compressed lips and tensed hands, as the struggle continues in dark bedrooms and sweat permeates the air of the village.

The same counterposing of elements is achieved on a collective level in the chapter "The Northerners" by juxtaposing brief sections of anonymous dialogue. The first, a rapid-fire series of unidentified fragments of gossip, sums up the popular resentment against these innovators for the attitudes, dress, and morality which they introduce upon returning home.

"It's worse when they come back," most people say. "Even the money they've earned doesn't do them any good." "And if it did, they're not satisfied here any more." "Many of them don't want to work any more; they just strut around, air their opinions, and criticize everything." "They're a bad example, poking fun at religion, the country, the customs." "They sow doubt, undermine people's love for working the land, and encourage them to leave this 'filthy, poverty-stricken country.' " "They're the ones who have brought in ideas of masonry, Socialism, and Spiritism. . . . To sum it up, they're a bunch of traitors. I don't know whether they know it or not, but the fact is they serve as the advance scouts of the gringos, to take away the land we have left, what they couldn't steal the other time."

In direct contrast, a long rebuttal follows. An unnamed "Northerner," speaking to the liberal-minded Father Reyes, catalogues the restraints which Mexican village life entails. Comparing them with what he has seen across the border, he prefigures the future when, for better or for worse, the under-dogs will insist on change.

"No, *Padre,* I'm sorry to say so, but when we come back, we realize what the people have to put up with, the injustice, and the bad conditions. Why should a man have to sweat all day to earn a few pennies? And sometimes not even that. Those rich ones can mix things up good, juggle your accounts, hold you off with enough corn and beans so you won't starve, and then just say, 'we'll see, at harvest time, next year.' . . . I tell you, *Padre,* it can't go on like this; sooner or later, the poor people are going to get fed up, and one way or another things will have to change. . . . This situation can't keep on. Oh, I agree that nobody here dies of hunger, but don't tell me that most people are doing more than barely living. . . . But go to Cuernavaca, Puebla, Chihuahua, where I worked, and you'll really see hell on earth, on the sugar farms and the huge *haci-endas.* The people live worse than slaves. . . . Here they don't know what's going on in other parts of the country. When the Revolution starts it will catch us un-awares."

Given its setting in the immediacy of revolution, *The Edge of the Storm* clearly carries an implication of historical causality. However, the novel's view of history is dialectical, and more complex than that of *Sunburst.* The interpretation of past events, on the one hand as repetitious and therefore a guide to knowledge of the present, on the other as portents of cataclysmic change, is embodied in the character Lucas. An old man whose role in the village is that of oral chronicler and guardian of the record of past occurrences, Lucas maintains mental accounts of all births and deaths, marriages and misfortunes; he amiably narrates family and village history at wakes, and provides a sense of continuity with the past. Further, he analyzes long-dead events and hints at their applications to the present. In this sense, through Lucas, the present repeats and incarnates past experience.

However, the old man is aware not only of village instability but of the increasingly strident tenor of disturbances throughout Mexico. His keen nose for news fastens on the scent of Madero, whose physical description he repeats over and over, fascinated. Toward the novel's end, Lucas perceives that his knowledge of the past signals only new and unpredictable terrors for the future. His deathbed admonition to Father Dionisio contains a warning:

> "We're on the edge of the storm! Look after yourself: no matter what happens, don't be troubled, *Padre;* it will be quite a deluge, and the first hailstones will hit you. Be strong!"

Lucas is an authentic character, expressive in his language and distinctive in his personality. Within the novel he is vital to the sequence of events and the internal structure. His role as the interpreter of the dialectics of history is successful because it stems from novelistic technique.

The structure of *The Edge of the Storm* converts the progression of time into a more complex phenomenon than mere lineal sequence, even though the narrative follows a defined chronological order, from the Lenten season of 1909 to the Madero revolt in November 1910. Chapters and events are related to this general progression as the tempo of the novel builds up—the whole of the 1910 portion being treated in one long, fast-moving, final chapter.

But there are moments when Yáñez finds nonchronological sequence vital to the development of a particular theme or set of relationships. Chapter continuity, shifting from one plot thread to another, and alternating between group and individual focus, frequently restructures temporal order and transcends its limitations. The sequence from chapters ten through thirteen provides an interesting example. "Holy Cross Day," chapter ten, is set on May 2 and May 3, 1909. Its multiple scenes capture simultaneously the status of various relationships at that time: the first physical contact between Damián and Micaela, and the final brief encounter of Victoria and Gabriel. Interspersed are scenes describing the town's pilgrimage to the Mission Cross on a nearby hill, underlining the biblical quality of the village customs of worship, and the highly significant dream of Don Dionisio, the thematic echoes of which resound in subsequent developments.

Chapter eleven, centering on Father Islas, continues until the end of June, when the fanatic chaplain has a heated interview with Damián on the subject of Micaela. The following chapter, "Ascension," reverts to Gabriel and Victoria, narrating the sorrowful reaction which her departure produces in Gabriel. It spans from May 6 through May 20. Chapter thirteen picks up the Damián-Micaela thread from chapter eleven (and from earlier references which had already predicted its outcome) and recounts the events of July and August—the murder and its aftermath.

Thus, several plot lines progress at the same time. Each moves according to its own rhythm, the connections and interrelationships depending on the reader. Within the overall objective framework of historical time, temporal progression is subjectivised, having one pattern and meaning for one set of characters, and a different value and rhythm for another. The reader is called upon to reorder these sequences.

Time and history, individual and group characters—
all of which comprise the substance of reality in *The Edge of
the Storm*—are analyzed in terms of their component, often
contradictory, elements. By these techniques, Yáñez sets up a
view of life as a tenuous balance between opposing pressures.
The omnipresent tension imparts depth to the novel's events
and characterizations.

CHARACTERIZATION

The question of characterization can be approached
from two standpoints—the group and the individual. The
former, involving the various techniques by which Yáñez
defines his own town-protagonist, has already been pointed
out and will be treated further in the following section with
relation to setting.

If this were the only effort at characterization in the
novel, the village would then be endowed with the same *typical* values found in earlier novels of the Revolution. Indeed,
an introductory comment by the author states that the work
might also have been entitled, "In a Village of the Archdio-
cese," for its action occurs in a Guadalajara town "whose
name it is not worth remembering." In this way, the author
avoids localization, allowing his work to acquire an emblem-
atic quality so that its implications may be more broadly applicable.

It is the second, complementary level of individual
characterization which particularizes the town, without reducing its illustrative effect. Although none is a central protagonist, a number of figures are highly developed, seen frequently in detail, and at times from within. Having furnished
a close-up view of their makeup, the narrator, in a change
of focus, can step back to see the village as though from afar,

integrating the sharper portrait of a moment before into a larger context.

Don Dionisio Martínez, parish priest, is a fundamental character in *The Edge of the Storm*. His personal destinies, which dramatize the multifaceted role of the church, parallel the town's fortunes, and his personality influences all the other important figures in the narrative. Dispersed across the changing pattern of plot relationships, at times submerged from view, the fullness of Don Dionisio as a character is not immediately self-evident, but must be recomposed by the reader. In the process, a profoundly tragic figure emerges.

Don Dionisio is introduced as a full-blown character, early in the novel. In a conventional portrait which supplies more information about him than does all of *The Underdogs* about its protagonist, Demetrio Macías, Yáñez traces the conscientious priest's concern for the failings of his parishioners, describes his moral structure, his physical appearance, and his biography prior to 1909, and sketches the ascetic regularity of his daily duties. A basis is thereby provided for understanding the changes which Don Dionisio will undergo as he faces the climactic events of the coming months, the turning point of his life.

The scope of change becomes evident as he is seen from various perspectives. One view is his behavior in response to the village's needs, prompted by unswerving adherence to his role as spiritual guide, storms and crises notwithstanding. In the face of rumors about secret Masonic and cultist groups, he increases his inquisitorial vigilance in the confessional, to ferret out the information. Tormented by the fear that his absence may expose his flock to temptation, he rises from his sickbed and on the verge of collapse conducts mass. While the shocked villagers advocate merciless punishment for Damián, Don Dionisio doggedly visits with him repeatedly, in an attempt to save a murderer's soul. On another occasion the incorruptible *padre* resists the blandishments of a venal political delegate who is anxious to shore up the tottering stance of the federal government by means of a status quo alliance with the church.

A second focus on the parish priest is evident in the middle course he steers between tactical pressures from the "right" and the "left"— from the fanatical Father Islas who would extirpate sexuality from human behavior and thought, and from the liberal Father Reyes, with ideas of social reforms and modern religious practices. The polar opposition between extreme overzealousness and doctrinal flexibility provides shadings which define the position of Don Dionisio.

His impact on other characters sheds further light on his nature. His heavy-handed repression of his niece, for whom he feels tender love, produces her frustration and ultimate rebellion. For the bell-ringer Gabriel, also raised by Don Dionisio in an aura of religious orthodoxy and over-protective kindness, his influence proves again to be essentially negative and repressive. Gabriel's love for María and the impulse for artistic expression which Victoria ignites in him are thwarted by the priest's insistence upon rigid morality. Yet for Father Reyes, Don Dionisio is an inspiration. The older man treats Reyes with a firm kindness and trust he had never known before, providing moral guidance by his own clear example of determination and rectitude. Again, by a revealing contrast, the multiple qualities of a strong character are displayed.

Complementing these outer manifestations of Don Dionisio's makeup, his inner life, open to the reader via narrative technique, provides the key to his psyche, for his mind is a battleground of contending forces. The novel follows the gradual disintegration of his confidence in an iron-disciplined system of orthodox values, as one after another of his charges rejects the teachings of the church.

In opposition to an outwardly austere rigidity, his internal conflict is conveyed by a dream in which those he loves are contaminated with sin—for which he feels himself responsible. Interior monologues reveal his increasing burden of guilt, and his doubts about himself and even about God. Striving for self-purification, he resorts to the medieval recourse of flagellation. Yet he stands by his religious commitment, and imposes his conscious will upon his subconscious doubt. It is this fierce inner struggle which imparts dramatic value to his courage, despite the fact that his thoughts are conveyed in language notable for its stiffness and sentimentality because Yáñez was less at home with interior monologue than with other stylistic techniques.

On the other hand, the author successfully conveys the solemn rhythms of liturgical language which are a constant motif in Don Dionisio's reflections. An elaborated style reinforces the reader's perceptions of the priest's ingrained religiosity:

> Long before daybreak, before four o'clock, often at three, Don Dionisio is awake, his sleep routed by thronging visions of his parishioners. His waking thoughts embrace them all: the fallen, struggling on the threshold of sleep, their eyes full of burning sand . . . those whose dreams are of lust; those who will awake to their old sufferings, temptations and problems; those over whose heads, over whose souls, hangs the sword of Damocles . . . those condemned to suffer; half-hearted believers, the troublesome, the wayward.

They all claim his first thoughts, his first drowsy, wordy prayers. "Hail, Mary, Refuge of Sinners, conceived without sin. In the name of the Father, the Son, and the Holy Ghost." With arms outstretched, he enfolds them all in the gesture with which he crosses himself, and kneels down to kiss the floor. *"Pecavi, Domine, miserere mei; pecavi, Domine, miserere mei; pecavi, Domine, miserere mei; poenitet me pecasse: cupio emmendare quod feci."* He brings discipline cracking down across his shoulders, suffering for his own sins and for the sins of his people. Kneeling with forehead to the floor, he sings the hymn, *Veni Creator,* then repeats the *Actiones nostras quaesmus, Domine* and the penitential psalms, continuing the flagellation until the last word is uttered.

In effect, Yáñez views the authenticity of his character's Catholicism with compassion, even as he penetrates the weaknesses of its psychological underpinnings. As the novel runs its course, Don Dionisio emerges as a genuine martyr, driving with every fibre of his being to achieve the impossible—to reverse the thrusts of history and human nature. In the end he is broken. The final paragraphs—after the Revolution has irrevocably burst upon the village, motivating the flight of his cherished niece—find him hopelessly conducting mass. His worshippers, with hostile eyes, watch cruelly for the signs of his impending breakdown.

Don Dionisio is one of the most fully rounded characters in the Mexican novel. Genuinely complex, he transcends stereotype. Like all valid literary characters, the figure of the austere *padre* provokes in the reader's mind a search for meaning.

Of the many characters whose lives intersect that of

Don Dionisio, some are merely types and others are more fully developed. While each has a distinct role vis-à-vis the novel's plot and themes, Yáñez has developed his secondary characters in interesting sets and clusters. In some pairs there is a conscious comparison by an overlapping of shared characteristics—between María and Micaela, Micaela and Victoria, Damián and Rito. In other sets, there is a clear contraposition of opposite types—Marta against María, Reyes against Islas.

This suggestive blend of contrasts and parallels in character development is never overt. The reader must work out for himself the implied patterns of personality, patterns which reinforce novelistic structure on a level more subtle than the customary story line.

The key to character development in *The Edge of the Storm* is the focus on the interior life, for Yáñez is the first Mexican to apply Freudian principles to the novel. He introduced interior monologue, incorporated dreams into the fibre of the narrative, dealt more fully with sexual motivation, examined the role of the subconscious, and explored repression, expression, symbolism, and sublimation. In each of his important personages, the interplay of conscious and subconscious worlds determines the role, the characters and the town within the novel.

Yáñez also employs the technique of the case history, complete with symptoms and detailed descriptions of behavior. Two of his characters, driven by fear and guilt, lose all contact with reality and become psychotic. In the case of Luis Gonzaga, treated the more fully, Yáñez weaves in both the character's biography and a study of his personality as it disintegrates. Incoherent prayer and chaotic monologues, together with increasingly abnormal conduct, illuminate the onset of madness, with its roots in the conflicts between sexuality and religion. An account of his delusions and actions in the asylum describes the final stages of his psychosis.

The case of Father Islas is a more external study of behavior. His rabid obsession with sex is prefigured in the early "Acto preparatorio," although it is specifically identified later. Islas' authoritarian leadership of the Daughters of Mary, his extremely repressive guidance of spinsters and married women, his towering rage at Damián who seeks his blessing to pursue relations with Micaela, his compulsively hermetic personal routine—these are the components of his psychological profile. His ultimate collapse in a fit is a logical outcome. Within the novel, his psychological disintegration has the function of prefiguring and accentuating Don Dionisio's loss of confidence, marking the boundary between extreme sexual repression and insanity.

The incorporation of modern psychological knowledge by means of narrative technique is the essential literary element enabling Yáñez to fashion complex characters—a feature which markedly distinguishes *The Edge of the Storm* from the novel of the Revolution.

SETTING

Conceived in its broadest terms, the setting of *The Edge of the Storm* is one of its most distinctive features. Setting, the aura which surrounds and informs every facet of village existence, is most evident in the opaque backdrop before which the leading characters strive, against overwhelming odds, to find expression and meaning in their lives. The scope of these odds is increased by the essential hostility of the novel's setting, which encompasses cultural heritage, historical background, psychological climate, and economic and political composition, as well as the concrete geographical environment.

Opaqueness and hostility are subjective factors, and their presence is first felt in the "Acto preparatorio." Transcending the conventional introduction of place and time, this passage stylizes the elements of setting, establishing the active importance of village atmosphere through the process of attributing esthetic qualities to it. When characters are subsequently introduced in the first chapter, they are already enveloped in the aura of the "Acto." The treatment of setting, then, is an important vehicle for conveying the author's particular interpretation of the reality which confronts his characters. Established with artistic coherence, it is an indispensable dimension of *The Edge of the Storm,* without which the characters would be deformed. In fact, the substance of the novel is the partial breakdown of this initial setting. The final chapter, contrasting with the "Acto," depicts a village whose character, mood, beliefs, mode of existence, and connections with the outside world are all in a state of shock. The static, monotonous quality of the "Acto," with its echoes of medieval and biblical elementality, has been permanently altered, although neither erased nor replaced.

Tradition, in the sense of reliving the past, adhering to familiar cultural values, and rejecting innovation, plays a major role. Of all the aspects of traditionalism, religion is the dominant. Examination of its treatment, of how its environmental pressure is an integrated thread throughout the novel, demonstrates the larger presentation of setting.

As stated previously, religious practice and belief in the village underlie several major thematic conflicts: in Don Dionisio, the conflict between Christian ethics and basic human nature; in Mercedes, Damián, and Micaela, between restrictive social norms and personal freedom. Further, its omnipresence influences temporal sequence and, therefore, structure, since major chapters are built upon climactic moments in village life, and these are determined by the rhythm of the religious calendar.

Stylistic techniques communicate the pervasive quality of centuries-old orthodoxy in the village. The opening paragraphs, describing the austere appearance of the village, are constructed of static sentences, rhythmic and repetitious in their slow adjectival accumulation of sounds and visual characteristics, but unusual for the absence of verbs. The effect is one of quiescence, motionlessness, permanence. A baroque prose style, with majestic elaboration and patterning, is also notable in descriptions of the interior torment of Luis Gonzaga and of the hyperemotional reaction in the town upon experiencing the novelty of popular music. In both cases, one individual, the other collective, the full description serves to search out every shading and detail of emotion, as inner feelings clash with the clerical practice.

Yáñez frequently endows his prose with musicality. The village bells are a constant leitmotif, whose absence or distortion, as on the occasion of Gabriel's grief, have a disturbing effect on the townspeople. On Easter Monday, when Victoria is struck by the spiritual force of Gabriel's playing for the second time, the prose which describes her reaction conveys in its diction and rhythm the esthetic qualities of sacred music. Her feelings, equating death and pain with a sensation of voluptuous enjoyment, are reinforced by soaring, romantic images and the repetition of a central phrase, "Beyond the bounds of Death," which in Spanish ("A través de la Muerte") has a rhythm which might suggest the heaving peal of church bells.

She was filled with overwhelming tenderness. It was as if she felt anew all the griefs experienced in this and many former lives, as if in this moment, when her very foundations were shaken, she could feel again the sufferings of even her most remote ancestors. In her veins coursed the pulsing joys and sorrows of countless men and women, buried under the layers of centuries, communicating with her across time, beyond the bounds of Death. She was so moved that the burden of these reborn emotions was a fearful pleasure. Beyond the bounds of Death. An immeasurable joy never before imagined. Beyond the bounds of Death. A joy unexampled in her dreams or her experience of intellectual and physical pleasures. Travel, celebrations, friendship, intimate relationships; no, never had she imagined such pleasure. And pain. Pain strong enough to cause instant death. A pain of emptiness. Beyond the bounds of Death. As though when the bells began to toll, mournfully, musically, she had begun to fall, and were falling, falling into the dreaded void. Beyond the bounds of death. Solemn bells, like an organ—beyond the bounds of Death—played by the empty winds, by winds laden with eternity. An organ played by Death himself.[4]

For Victoria, as this passage ends, the unknown bell-ringer is endowed with the powers of the Archangel of Death, a religious symbol which presides over her attraction to Gabriel. It should be added that the subsequent buildup of this attraction, particularly at the moment of their first encounter, goes to a romantic extreme which stretches artistic coherence into the realms of emotional melodrama.

One visual effect of the town's pervasive religiosity is generated by the motif of the black-robed women, young and old, who daily dress as though in mourning. Repeated throughout the novel, this sombre image of female asceticism is finally broken, momentarily and forcefully, when María and the widow of Lucas González join the revolutionary maelstrom garbed in patterned dresses. But the emotive power of the novel's terse opening sentence, "Village of black-robed women," still characterizes the town María leaves behind her.

The living presence of biblical values and symbols is produced by numerous suggestive references. A description on Good Friday: "Village proud of its resemblance to Jerusalem, which was confirmed by a missionary who came from the Holy Land. Because of its desolate landscape. Because of its air of lamentation. Village of crosses!"

The same quality is evident in Victoria's evocation of the Archangel of Death and the Four Horsemen of the Apocalypse upon hearing the bells, and in Luis Gonzaga's tormented self-identification with Christ on the cross. The Retreat House, where men of the village annually spend a week of physical and mental self-castigation, is detailed as background for the "Exercises" which embody the apocalyptic fervor of the Mexican baroque period:

The walls—wherever the eyes turn . . .—are covered with vivid pictures and inscriptions which command attention and induce further meditation. Classical texts and popular verse, easy to remember; paintings of awe-inspiring realism: huge Stations of the Cross adorn the walls of the chapel and over the Altar are intensely dramatic sculptured figures of the Crucifixion, against a terrifying background of livid black clouds, lightning flashes streaking a desolate countryside, and a cluster of reddish houses representing hapless Jerusalem; allegories cover walls of the passageways, amid persistent inscriptions, leaving almost no empty space, with their gloomy, jarring colors. Here the death of a sinner, there the separate hells of the lustful, the miserly, the proud . . . farther along a body in decomposition, where the painter has delighted in the presence of worms which seem live, stuck to the canvas, bent on their gruesome task. On the central dividing wall . . . a painting of the Day of Judgment, fearful even to those who have often contemplated it . . . Eyes, overwrought souls come away from the terrible words resounding in the chapel: Death, Judgment, Heaven, Hell—and pass from the terrible inscriptions in large letters to confront the terrible paintings. They find no point of repose in their struggle against desire and sin, not even in sleep, for even there the impressions of their ordeal float, disembodied.

The above examples establish Mexican Catholicism as a living atmospheric element, continually interacting with the consciousness of the villagers. A key aspect of the relationship between man and the religious component of his cultural environment in *The Edge of the Storm* is its two-way character. The hostile, largely negative influences exerted by religious practice and tradition are themselves caused by and related to man. Further, individual reactions to these environmental pressures vary from character to character. The same can be said of the various individual interactions with other elements in the overall atmosphere—historical, political, economic, even geographical. Environment, hostile though it may be, is no longer an abstract, monolithic force which uniformly determines individual destinies. Now it is seen as created and influenced by man, in a novel which moves away from determinism and places a premium on the complexity of human nature.

WORLD VIEW

Ambivalence is a quality that sets *The Edge of the Storm* apart from its predecessors as a landmark novel. *The Underdogs* contends that the Revolution betrayed its declared goals, that instead of replacing injustice with humanity, the conflagration unleashed the worst features in a sin-ridden nation. Implicit are moral judgments against the characters, the Revolution, the nation. Yáñez, on the other hand, speaks from greater distance. He offers no final judgment, but examines with objectivity and sympathy the inevitable clash between outmoded institutions and human nature.

This is especially true in the characterization of Don Dionisio. Within an anticlerical context, Yáñez is able to humanize—even to convert into a minor antihero—a character whose entire being depends upon his commitment to uphold the backward aspects of obsolete religious institutions. We sympathize with the priest's concern for his flock while we witness the dire effects of that concern. It is this ambivalence that carries the book beyond the bounds of narrow nationalism to themes of universal interest.

Dialetical antithesis is another characteristic of the outlook of *The Edge of the Storm,* again new to the Mexican novel. In the prior works discussed, brutality replaced brutality, corruption spawned corruption, and new oppression replaced old oppression. The circle was closed in upon itself.

But the vision of existence engendered in that unnamed Jalisco village—both past and present—enabled Yáñez to transcend this simplistic thesis and project toward an open-ended future. We can be certain, as we close the novel, that the trajectory of the village through the Revolution will be marked by new forms of the same tensions and contradictions whose moods, tenses, and inflections have been conjugated for us. Nevertheless, while the black-robed women remain, María departs; a change has occurred. The village will never be the same, but neither is the past eradicated.

The Edge of the Storm is anticlerical in tone, but not antireligious, again indicating a greater complexity of world view. The anticlericalism lies in a sense of the utter inadequacy of blind, fanatical dogmatism which affirms the hegemony of death and guilt over life and love. It is devastating in its evaluation of anachronistic practices which repress the individual and impose fear rather than faith, in effect generating anguish. But at the same time, its dualistic approach makes possible a sensitive view of authentic religiosity beneath the overlay of extremism, and an appreciation of the undeniable weight of traditions inherited over centuries. Yáñez communicates the esthetics of religious symbols, even those which damage his characters. He explores humanistic elements such as the Song of Songs and the poetry of Fray Luis de León, blending them into his introduction of Gabriel, to explain the rapture which religion-inspired music inspires in the primitive bell-ringer. Through the personage of Father Reyes, the author establishes a link between national spirit and the cult of the Virgin of Guadalupe—a link which shows a positive though ephemeral reconciliation of religion and nationalism. But as the storm breaks, reconciliation is broken. Like the Revolution, the thrust of *The Edge of the Storm* was strongly anticlerical.

Another new facet of Yáñez' view is a changed relationship of individual to social forces. No longer in *The Edge of the Storm* does man find himself completely at the mercy of events, nor does his fate depend solely on exterior pressures. It is the introduction of Freudian psychology that enlarges the author's viewpoint. We are presented with a modern interpretation of man, capable of moving irrepressibly toward assertion—sexual, artistic, political. Without omitting social and cultural context, the author delves into the subsurface of his characters. Man's subjective character now can be discerned as an important source, and possible solution, of his problems.

The added dimension of individualization through psychological development of character represents a considerable step beyond the earlier novels, absorbed as they were in the broad effects of a sweeping social conflagration, concerned with the human forest as a whole and unable to concentrate attention on particular differentiations among the trees.

Realism, from this standpoint, acquires new meaning, for Yáñez extends the definition of reality. Objectivity no longer depends upon capturing central aspects of observable existence, but upon the interaction between various subjective views of reality, and upon interplay between the whole and its parts.

In many ways, the historical present of the novel—1909 and 1910—is seen as the point of intersection of two relentless pressures: the weight of past tradition versus the imminence of revolutionary change. But just as the past is a

summation of contradictory forces, the future implied in the
narrative is composed of a rearrangement rather than a complete reversal and rejection of the past. *The Edge of the
Storm* projects a redefinition of the terms of contention, not
the elimination of black by white.

Since the novel itself consists of a retrospective glance
back in history—a sounding of the turbulent waters which
swelled into the flood of Revolution—it clearly offers a study
of causality so lacking in its literary antecedents. But the
author's dialectical approach has been overlooked by the
critics, and this has resulted in overly facile judgments. On
the one hand, Julieta Campos implies that the Revolution is
merely an external development, and that the parallel between
events in the village and those in the nation lacks validity, for
the village in effect is left untouched by the upheaval:

> But the village, the tiny community as a whole, is the
> negation of that yearning (for personal and collective
> liberation); it is static, an obstacle to historic happen-
> ings, and after the passage of the revolutionaries it re-
> mains once again as before, as always. Time in Yáñez
> is a monotonous flow, agitated only by the catastrophic.
> Despite the fact that the action occurs within a con-
> crete historical framework, the definite impression re-
> ceived is one of stagnation, not of dynamism.[5]

Similarly, Victor Flores Olea separates the town from the
Revolution, adducing as evidence the fact that today, with
the Revolution having run its course, there are villages in
Mexico which live and breathe the reality of *The Edge of
the Storm:*

> . . . I couldn't help but be concerned over the contem-
> porary quality and the living presence of Yáñez' world.

After fifty years of history—a long time after . . .
the storm convulsed our society—we still find, with
alarming frequency, villages and lives which are identical to those in the novel. What happened to that storm
for it to leave unaltered the most profound strata of
Mexican life? What happened to the Revolution so that
despite having changed . . . the face of the nation, it
left without noticeable transformation the life and customs of those little towns?

. . . . .

. . . Yáñez describes for us a social and human reality
that could not be changed by *that* storm, by *that* Revolution. He uncovers its most intimate workings, its motivations, the causes of its 'stability.' And we can understand the reasons for the permanence and immobility
of . . . Mexican villages.

. . . . .

. . . Yáñez, in this way, comes to grips with the question, *why,* socially and morally, for each one of those
people, the storm could not change the form and
rhythms of life; why the wind of the Revolution was incapable of modifying the ancient régime of these customs, these modes of being. Drawing close to his characters, and making us take a close look at ourselves,
Yáñez lays bare the causes of that resistance . . . And
the reasons by which the old régime continues, in good
part, to be the régime in power.[6]

In an opposite sense, other commentators find indications of a purifying revolution which will completely sweep
away the reality of the novel. José Vázquez Amaral speaks
of impending transfiguration:

Thus Yáñez introduces, through the fortunate medium

of human symbols who perturb us because their makeup is too demoniacal to be human, the supernatural figures of Gabriel and Victoria. They announce for us the coming of fire and blood, and finally, of the transfiguration of the Mexican nation.[7]

Following this line of reasoning, Elaine Haddad also assumes that revolution in the novel portends something akin to complete change: ". . . The obvious reason for the details of the major part of the novel is to show us what it is that the Revolution will sweep away."[8]

From literary elements alone, it is possible to discern a coherent though mixed set of implications within *The Edge of the Storm* concerning the Revolution.[9] For Don Dionisio, certainly, it represents a major tragedy, as it does also for the anonymous chorus of women in black. The latter remain, defeated, defensive, and hostile, and clearly will not be converted into supporters of the new social forces. Damián, Rito, and María, on the other hand, find liberation in the breaking storm. They are free to follow its turbulence. But certainly within the village itself the relationship of power must change, with the "Northerners" in the ascendancy, able to impose new social, cultural, and economic norms upon the formerly church-dominated semifeudal community.

The entire structure of the narrative takes into account the parallel between the village situation and that of the nation. Hermetic though its existence may be, the interior life of the village responds to multiple stimuli from outside, converting these responses into local expressions. Just as the supporters of Madero explode inevitably against repression, so too are María and others galvanized into dynamic insistence on freedom. But the parallel applies conversely too. The black-robed women still inhabit the village, and their sombre presence will brake the thrust for transformation, limiting its scope. On a larger scale, too, the Revolution will soon be contained throughout the nation.

Although Yáñez was not primarily concerned with the historical projection of *The Edge of the Storm*, its very coherence—the mood, characters, and structure of its literary world—assumes a visible attitude toward the Revolution. A guarded, relatively optimistic evaluation is inherent in his drama.

Yáñez is the first Mexican author who consciously transcends narrow literary nationalism, finding it no longer adequate to the demands of the modern novel. While his work is an examination of the national past, the themes and techniques are universal. Revolution by his treatment is not merely a Mexican phenomenon, but is bound up with such universal categories as the psychological structure of personality and the fundamental antithesis between repression and expression as the basis for ethical and moral norms.

He not only applies European concepts, such as those of Freudian psychology, and a view of reality which seems based in Hegelian dialectics and contemporary relativism, but also imparts a sense of literary form and craftsmanship. Toward this goal, he approached his work with a considerably broader acquaintance with world literature than his predecessors possessed.

Yáñez himself has stated his conscious interest in Dos Passos while writing *The Edge of the Storm:* "I sought the way to apply to a small village the techniques Dos Passos uses to describe the big city in *Manhattan Transfer.*"[10] As Octavio Paz has observed, Yáñez not only learned the interior monologue from Joyce, but shared with him a number of attitudes:

Joyce was a decisive example for Agustín Yáñez. I say example and not influence, although he may have been both one and the other, because the key point was not the assimilation of certain techniques but the attitude toward reality: Catholic tradition and bare realism; preference for the pageantry of language and the labyrinths of the conscience; a hunger of the senses and a taste of ashes on lips; and finally, a certain amorous ferocity toward the place of birth.[11]

Shunning traditional emphasis on anecdotal elements and withdrawing from the immediacy of a thesis, Yáñez moved in the direction of literary self-reliance. Artistic autonomy, a universal outlook, the perception of reality as complex and ambiguous, authentic psychological probing— these are the qualities which make *The Edge of the Storm* the turning point in Mexican fiction.

JUAN RULFO, one of the least prolific writers on the contemporary scene, has published just one novel and one collection of short stories, *El llano en llamas* (México, 1953). The latter volume was made available in English, with the title *The Burning Plain and Other Stories*, by the University of Texas Press in 1967, as part of its excellent series of Latin American fiction.

Born in 1918, Rulfo is a native of Jalisco. But here the similarity with Yáñez ends abruptly. Rulfo's childhood was in the arid, infertile, semideserted region of southern Jalisco which serves as the setting for his stories and for *Pedro Páramo*. His family was decimated by the *cristero* wars, church-led rebellions against the government in 1926-1928. As a boy, he was passed on to an orphanage in Guadalajara, where he received a minimal education which petered out by the time he was fifteen. Subsequently, after gravitating to Mexico City and securing the first of many nondescript government jobs, he sporadically attended literature classes of the National University. But the bulk of his education, and his widespread knowledge of world literature, came through his own voracious appetite for reading.

At present, in addition to his editorial work for the National Indian Institute, Rulfo serves with Juan José Arreola as adviser and mentor to the young authors who hold fellowships at the government- and foundation-endowed Mexican Writers' Center. Since the publication of *Pedro Páramo* in 1955, he has been preparing another novel, entitled *La cordillera*, but is unwilling to see it in print, despite publishers' pressure, until he feels completely satisfied.

3 | THROUGH THE WINDOW OF THE GRAVE: JUAN RULFO

Pedro Páramo

"I came to Comala because I was told that my father, a certain Pedro Páramo, was living there."[1] So starts Rulfo's novel of rural Jalisco, deceptively simple and so different from the Yáñez work that the contrast is itself illuminating.

Rulfo found such elements as the dynamic progression of history and the complexities of Freudian psychology to be nonessential baggage. Appropriate to his *weltanschauung*, his narrative technique shuns a sequence that might relate causality to progression in time, and his depiction of character is almost bare of interior conflicts.

Rulfo finds the key to human nature elsewhere. He approaches the opaque side of man's psyche, where the dark imponderables reside: "Why does the world press in on us from all sides, and break us into pieces, and water the ground with our blood? What have we done? Why have our souls rotted?" It is this zone, timeless and static as Greek tragedy, which in his view decides the vagaries of man's encounter with fate.

How to distill this bitter poetic vision into novelistic form? The author's choice of ingredients is a paradoxical combination of highly stylized folk language on the one hand, and, on the other, a daringly complex structure which deliberately confounds the reader in its mazelike obscurity. At moments it is scarcely prose. "He heard the weeping. That woke him up, that soft, thin sound of weeping, perhaps because it was so thin it could slip through the mazes of sleep to the place where the fears dwell." The result is a sensitive Mexican variation on the tragic immutability of man's anguish.

The nature of incident in *Pedro Páramo* is difficult to describe, because Rulfo fragments his narrative into tiny divisions (there are no chapters) which are more often than not unrelated to each other in time or place, and are populated by diverse characters who are rarely introduced and almost always difficult to identify. The reader must strain for connections, and is compelled to construct events and identities in order to wrest meaning from apparent disarray.

The novel begins in retrospective first person with an account by Juan Preciado of his arrival at Comala. On her deathbed his mother had urged him to seek out Pedro Páramo, the father who had abandoned them. He finds Comala an infernal ghost town—dry, seared, and empty except for a few mysterious individuals. Most, or all of these creatures —it slowly becomes clear—are in fact dead, though their memories of Juan's mother and Pedro Páramo are still vivid.

Interspersed with the boy's strange encounters are sections of remembered speech which present his mother's description of Comala. Her images of pastoral fecundity contrast with the arid lifelessness which Juan encounters.[2] Other sections, at first inexplicable, introduce the memories of Pedro Páramo, recounted both in first-person musings and in dialogue of scenes which he recalls.

A vision of Pedro Páramo begins to emerge, but only tenuously, for identities are often in doubt. Gradually it becomes apparent that Juan is communicating with the spirits of dead people whose bodies are interred while their souls are condemned to roam the earth. Midway in the narrative, Juan tells of his own death and burial. By this time, various moments in the life of Pedro Páramo have been described from one source or another: his childhood love for Susana San Juan, his assumption of the family's debt-ridden ranch, his revenge of the gratuitous murder of his father, and his relentless ascent to power. One of Pedro's least violent methods of building an empire was marriage to Dolores Preciado (who later was Juan's mother) in order to possess her land.

The death of Pedro's illegitimate, wastrel son Miguel also figures in the narrative. Miguel is thrown from his horse during a nocturnal escapade in search of women. Earlier, he had murdered the brother of the village priest Padre Rentería, and had seduced the niece of this hesitating, guilt-ridden cleric. The latter, aware of Miguel's depredations, and of Pedro's evil grip upon the region, is rendered impotent by his own weakness.

Although these are the narrative threads of the first half, they reach the reader indirectly. The story seems to center on Juan's encounter with the unreal atmosphere of Comala—his strange meetings with living-dead characters and with a few funereal ones who appear to be alive, and the random, unexplained rememberings of Pedro Páramo, emanating from a source unidentified in time and place.

The central narrative device of the second half consists of dialogues from the tomb, between Juan and the old woman Dorotea, with whom he lies buried. It now becomes clear to a startled reader that Juan's earlier first-person remembrances were also part of this exchange between two dead characters. A further narrative medium is the series of monologues which Juan overhears from the adjacent grave, where Susana San Juan lies twisting and turning, remembering the past. As in the first half, there are also sections recounted in third person by an unknown narrator.

The diverse fragments continue to develop the fortunes of Pedro Páramo, whose epic stature as *cacique* is matched only by his obsessed love for Susana. The latter had left Comala as a child, but Pedro Páramo, throughout his rise to power, had sought news of her, keeping track of her marriage and subsequent widowhood. With characteristic ruthlessness, he invited her father to return with Susana, and then urged him off to a prearranged death. Susana, left behind, was to consummate the crowning desire of the *cacique*. Having felt genuine passion in her marriage, however, Susana rejects further participation in life, seeking refuge in madness. In this state she can take solace from remembered moments of sensual joy, withdrawing totally from Pedro's love and from Padre Rentería's pressure for remorse. Within the novel, she is the only figure whose memories include a minimal glimpse of happiness, although significantly it is happiness encased in insanity.

Simultaneous with the frustration of Pedro's lifelong desires is the advent of the Revolution, which serves secondarily to relate events to the chronology of the outside world. Through bribery and sagacious maneuvering, Pedro manages to ride the waves of the upheaval. His tactic is to ally himself with spontaneously risen bands of rebels, providing men and a minimum of help, and channeling their marauding to adjacent villages.

The ensuing death of Susana is not mourned in Comala. Indeed, the incessant bells attract the curious from miles around, and initial expressions of grief slowly give way to a riotous fiesta. Angered and embittered, Pedro Páramo swears to avenge himself by allowing the village to go to waste.

This promise he fulfills, passing the remainder of his days on his ranch, in stolid meditation by the side of the road, calling forth the memories which have appeared throughout the novel and which now take on meaning in the context of his impending death. The final scene is that of Pedro's demise at the hands of the drunken Abundio, grief-stricken at the death of his own wife. The scene is tinged with double irony, for Abundio is Pedro's illegitimate son, who in his drunken state does not even recognize his father.

This brief resumé places into orderly relationship the anecdotal substance of the novel—the story that is told. More important is the specific nature of the process—how it is communicated—for in the discussion of technique lie the clues to the literary uniqueness of *Pedro Páramo*. Point of view, structure, style, development of character, and a mythic substructure all combine to project special dimensions to an implicit world outlook.

NARRATIVE PERSPECTIVE

Essential to Rulfo's method of narration is the perspective from which he portrays people and events in his novelistic world. The fact that we learn from the first few pages that Pedro Páramo is dead, and that Comala is some sort of ghostly village, imposes a particular color upon the entire work. Indeed, by the second half, when it becomes clear that Juan himself is in the grave, the specter of death completes its earlier, tentative invasion of life.

Death as a narrative vantage point heightens the sense of inexorability. The fate of those whose lives are recalled is viewed from a perspective which reduces the importance of anecdote and conflict, since climax and resolution are cut off in advance.[3] Rather than being narrated as though brought to life, which is the case in most fiction, the essential contours of the story are uncovered as static, almost isolated phenomena seen from across a vast boundary in time. One could even say, seen from the timeless perspective of the afterlife. The loss of suspense which this procedure entails is compensated in the handling of structure.

A second function of narrative perspective is to create a tone of apparent objectivity, separating the author from his characters. Much of this effect is achieved by introducing a "witness" narrator, Juan Preciado, whom we follow as he gathers information about Pedro Páramo. Significantly, as Carlos Blanco Aguinaga has observed, Juan never evaluates or ponders on information, which the reader receives untouched by Juan's personal interpretation, and is forced to interpret for himself.[4] Also there are remembered occurrences, in which various characters, such as Eduviges, Damiana, Susana, describe particular events to Juan, most frequently in language which is brief, unsubjectivized and understated. Even the monologues and memories of Pedro Páramo perform a function which is largely narrative, rather than one of subjective self-analysis.

At various moments in the novel the author returns to an already known incident, approaching it from a new angle or point of view. This process of multiple focus rounds out the reader's apprehension of the events and their impact on various characters. An excellent example is the death of Miguel Páramo. First it is recounted in the magical-folk version of Eduviges, who recalls her conversation with the dead Miguel shortly after his fatal accident. Several pages later comes a report of the funeral mass, highlighting Padre Rentería's reactions: at first, moral condemnation of the sinful deceased, then acceptance of Pedro Páramo's financial donation and reversal of his earlier refusal to bless the body. In the second half of the novel, a third-person narration describes how Pedro Páramo was notified of the death, and how he reacted with the fatalistic observation, belying a sense of his own misdeeds: "I'm beginning to pay. Better to start early. You finish sooner." Immediately following are the memories of Padre Rentería which serve to explain the priest's deep guilt. The interlocking nature of these four sections establishes their credibility, allowing the reader to piece together some of the tiles of a mosaic which at first confuses him. The emphasis is not so much on the events themselves as on the interrelationships which the multiple foci illuminate.

Thus Rulfo employs a series of techniques which endow with apparent objectivity the narrative fragments of his novel. The dispassionate "witness" narrator; the nonjudgmental tone of other characters; the reinforcing nature of versions of the same set of events—all these dispose us to accept as truthful the accounts we receive of Rulfo's Comala. On the other hand, when placed in an order which permits synthetic interpretation, these components make up a total world which is far from clear and objective. The perspective of death, with its consequent nullification of temporal sequence and the logic of cause and effect, serves to attenuate reality and to affix a particularly subjective seal to the anguished world of *Pedro Páramo*.

The procedure reverses that of Yáñez, who analyzes through interior monologue, dreams, and descriptions of characters' thoughts their paradoxical subjective nature, enabling him, as Manuel de Ezcurdia has indicated, "to approach objective reality by means of many subjective impressions of diverse characters . . . ."[5] Rulfo discards realism entirely, seeking instead to make an overall subjective statement about the nature of man. Precisely because his goal is subjective, he resorts to the techniques of objectivity to carry the reader along.

STRUCTURE

The structure of *Pedro Páramo* is one of the aspects which immediately stands out as unique. Though it may make life difficult for the reader, its distinctiveness performs a vital role esthetically and conceptually within the novel.

The very first impression is perhaps related to the elemental, laconic style of the opening paragraphs, followed by the realization that all is not in traditional order in this first-person account by Juan Preciado. For one thing, on the second page, when he describes the road to Comala, another description is juxtaposed, in italics and in present tense:

> The road went up and down; *"it goes up and down depending on whether you're coming or going. If you're going away, it's uphill, but it's downhill if you're coming back."*

Half a page below, a similar passage appears, but now the voice in italics is identified as that of Juan's mother. The identification must be applied retroactively by the reader to the first fragment. This is the first taste of the interpolation of unexpected material. In this case, explanation is withheld only for one-half page, thus softening the impact.

The second, third, and fourth narrative sections concentrate, along with the first, upon the arrival of Juan in Comala, his initial impressions and his encounter with Eduviges Dyada—all initiating the reader into the novel's rarefied atmosphere. Gradually the customary foundations of time and substance are weakened: Pedro Páramo, Juan learns, is dead, although he is also termed "a living hate"; Comala is seen both as a ghost town and formerly fecund village; in its searing heat and airless atmosphere, Comala, it is suggested, is an infernal place; Eduviges, the first person Juan meets, seems to straddle the boundary between life and death, and the lodging she offers him seems strange; most important, she reveals foreknowledge of his coming, casually referring to notification by his dead mother.

This growing incomprehensibility produces in Juan a feeling of stupor and bewilderment—a sensation at least partly shared by the reader:

> I thought the woman must be crazy. Then I didn't think any thing at all. I felt like I was in a far-off

world, and I just let myself be carried along. My body seemed to be floating, it was so limp, and you could have played with it as if it were a rag doll.

At this declaration of psychological weightlessness, indicating the absence of normal bases for reckoning with time and reality, the full force of structural innovation is brought to bear. The next segment changes abruptly in characters and setting, providing no clues for the reader, who, indeed, for a moment is misled. It switches to a dialogue between Pedro Páramo as a boy and his mother. Injected suddenly into this interchange are fragments of the adult Pedro Páramo's memories of boyhood, and his early love for Susana, set off only by quotation marks. And then, after three of these narrative sections in four pages, the reader is suddenly jolted back to the speech of Eduviges, in dialogue with Juan. Soon there will be more sudden shifts.

Such is the labyrinthine pattern of narrative sequence, a pattern which does not vary, except that the death of Juan occasions a clear and natural division into two parts. The second part will now be narrated from the "present" of death, as he and Dorotea lie in their adjoining graves. Although it becomes clear that Juan really had been dead while narrating the first part, the author had good reason to withhold this information.

Juan's death actually serves as a dividing line between two perspectives of narration. Here structure and the technique of withholding information are related to the vision of reality. Emphasis was placed, in the first half, on an apparently live Juan with whom the reader could identify as he encountered death, in the form of the infernal mystery of Comala. The ghostly, cadaverous face of the town was perceived by one who seemed still to live, but whose vitality was increasingly sapped by the overwhelming impact of death on his senses.

The second half—more in emphasis rather than uniformly—reverses the process, and is a mirror image of the first. From the grave, Juan and Dorotea (and through Juan, Susana) now focus on the days when Comala was alive. Once again, despite the reversal of perspective, the same pessimistic premise is clear: death predominates over life. In the first half, the presence of death contaminates existence; life is a living hell. In the second half, life contaminates death, making that condition hell also.

In this static world the only thing that alters is the backdrop. We can, in fact, discern four stages in the process by which the impact of Pedro Páramo changes the landscape. First, out of the past, is the lyric beauty described in the memories of Dolores and Susana. Then, at about the time of Miguel's death, Padre Rentería tells his priest confessor: "I've tried to raise grapes in Comala. They don't bear. Only oranges and berries. Bitter oranges and bitter berries. I've forgotten what sweet things taste like."

Years later, when social disturbances of the impending 1910 Revolution compel his return, Susana's father describes Comala:

> "Some villages taste of bad luck. You can tell them by drinking a little of their stale air. It's poor and thin, like everything else that's old. This is one of those villages, Susana.
> "Back at La Andrómeda you could at least pass the time watching things being born: the clouds, the birds, the moss. Do you remember? But there isn't anything

here except that stale yellow smell wherever you go. The village is bad luck. Nothing but bad luck."

Clearly, the village is well on its way to total barrenness.

Finally, Pedro Páramo's death takes place against a physical background which corresponds to Rulfo's estimate of man's condition. The sterility which the name Páramo implies,[6] and which is the state Pedro dictated for Comala, is also his own fate, for of his three sons none is destined to survive or to have issue who survive. Miguel's capricious death occurs within the novel. Abundio, whose wife and infant son are dead, dies after killing his father, for it is his spirit which guides Juan to Comala. And Juan, we realize at the novel's end, will arrive at some subsequent point of time (the novel's beginning), committed to a search which will result in his death but will enable him to continue to reconstruct the tragedy of Pedro Páramo.

While the two halves of the novel switch their focus, as though the narration were projected by reversed lenses, the dominant element in both is death, whether the focus be on subject or object. In the first half it is Juan the narrator-subject whose devitalization we witness, against the background of the ghostly Comala he encounters. In the second half it is Susana and Pedro Páramo, and with them Comala—the objects of narrative interest—which move inexorably toward absorption into timelessness, while the state of the narrator remains suspended.

Structure plays a multiple role in contributing to the particular literary unity upon which *Pedro Páramo* is based. Most obvious is the fact that sudden narrative switches in time, place, and person destroy the normal process of tracing causality in its relation to the stately procession of events in temporal sequence. Certainly the reader will reorder the diverse fragments, striving to reconstruct chronology. Nevertheless, the novel's structure, which forces him to view occurrences *initially* out of real context, shunts his search for causality elsewhere.

Thus, for example, our estimate of Pedro Páramo is first formed by events which take place after his death. We are introduced to him through Juan's visit to the Comala strangled by Pedro Páramo, who is characterized on the fourth page as "a living hate." Juxtaposed with this posthumous view are contrasting flashbacks of Pedro's past: a fragment from his childhood, adolescent memories, then the sequences involving Miguel. The result of this apparently chaotic sequence is to isolate events and character from the flow of the world about them, thus muting the traditional interplay between man and his social and historical circumstance.

Structure also contributes to a nonsequential view of time. The dominant process in *Pedro Páramo* is neither development nor progression, but the revelation of finality— the static, permanent qualities inherent in human existence. Events flow backward and forward, with the future and present merged into the past.

Structure similarly helps to erode the divisions between reality and irreality, divisions which for Rulfo must be blurred in order to affirm the presence of mythic and magical elements in man's psyche.

Esthetically, the mazelike form stands in contraposition to the elementality of its language. This interplay between simplicity and complexity is a distinct new quality in the Mexican novel. Certainly, the contrast with *The Edge of the Storm* is striking. Yáñez relied on a structure which, if not simple, was orderly and time-related, while major attention was paid to stylistic elaboration marked by profusion and reiterative patterns. It is not surprising that *Pedro Páramo* is less than one-third the length of the earlier novel.

Mystery is another attribute to which structure contributes. Bewilderment of the reader is substituted for the suspense which frequently accompanies plot or character development. An example of this technique is the withholding of the name of the first person narrator, Juan Preciado, until page forty-six. If, when this fact is finally provided in passing, the reader notices it, he is then able to establish the relationship between Juan and the Dolores Preciado who had been lured into marriage by Pedro Páramo. Further, he can recall with new meaning a different version of the wedding night which had been provided earlier by Eduviges.

Jean Paul Sartre was aware of this type of procedure in Faulkner, and his comments on *Sartoris* are in many ways transferable to Rulfo's novel.

> There is a formula: not to tell, to remain silent, disloyally silent—to tell *just a little*. We are told furtively (some information). . . . Furtively, in a phrase that risks passing unnoticed, and which it is hoped will pass *almost* unnoticed. After which, when we expect storms, we are shown instead just gestures, in long and minute detail. Faulkner is aware of our impatience, he counts on it . . . . From time to time, as though negligently, he unveils a consciousness for us . . . . Only what there is *within* this consciousness he doesn't tell us. It is not that he wants precisely to hide it from us: he wants us to guess it for ourselves, because guessing renders magical whatever it touches.[7]

Closely related is the question of reader involvement. Just as in the above example, we are called upon to make connections, the essence of Rulfo's technique is to deny his own omniscience, compelling us to share his own imperfect view of reality, and to supplement it if we can.[8] Indeed, Rulfo goes to the extreme of setting out snares which entrap us, first into confusion, then into esthetic reward if we were able to find our way.

The Presentation of Character

The figure of Pedro Páramo is both poetic image and flesh-and-blood character in his embodiment of tragedy. Carlos Blanco Aguinaga has indicated the fundamental lines of Rulfo's character presentation:

> Among this world of people-echoes, Pedro Páramo is the only one in whom the double dimension of character is well delineated: with his own life outwardly— individuality—and his own life of interior illusion— personality.[9]
>
> *   *   *   *   *
>
> Through Susana San Juan, Pedro Páramo attains the double level of a complete character which the others do not have in the novel. And it is this double level, the tension created in him by two opposed human planes (exterior violence, dreamy interior lassitude) which makes of Pedro Páramo a character of tragic dimensions. All his violence and his cold exterior cruelty are no more than the vain effort to conquer the impregnable fortress of his interior dream and pain.[10]

Blanco Aguinaga also observes that the two levels of character are isolated one from the other and do not influence each other until the end of the narrative when the *cacique* renounces his life of dynamic activity after Susana's death. Further, the contrast between interior sensitivity and exterior hostility is present as a consistent phenomenon, in the boy as well as the man. There is no significant change or evolution in Pedro Páramo.

Not only does the protagonist fail to evolve, in the traditional manner of the "round" character, his personality and individuality are discernible only in the barest, most essential terms. The scope of his interior life is limited to his love for Susana, in brief flashes which are magnified because there is no competing glimpse of other areas of his psyche, and because of their concentrated lyricism. An early passage captures the paradoxical sensitivity of an otherwise brutal man:

> "I was thinking of you, Susana. In the green hills. When we flew kites in the windy season. We heard the sounds of the village down below us while we were up there, up on the hill, and the wind was tugging the string away from me. 'Help me, Susana.' And gentle hands grasped my hands. 'Let out more string.'
>
> "The wind made us laugh; our glances met while the string paid out between our fingers; but it broke, softly, as if it has been struck by the wings of a bird. And up there the paper bird fell in somersaults, dragging its rag tail, until it was lost in the green of the earth.
>
> "Your lips were moist, as if they had been kissing the dew."

The performance of Pedro Páramo in the world around him, conveyed in terms of its impact on others and therefore obliquely described, is also narrated in fragments which concentrate only on the highlights necessary to apprehend the full force of his destructiveness.

The result of this characterization process is a figure of giant size but still a "people echo," as Blanco Aguinaga so aptly stated. One might also describe Pedro Páramo as a silhouette—all black and white with no grey areas. His transcendental conflict is reduced to its barest essentials: violence, arrogance, and lust versus love and sensibility to beauty.

Pedro Páramo is the center of the novel, the figure who shapes and defines others. He achieves vast proportions because he incarnates the elemental nature of myth, because he is an abstraction, an essence. His tragedy can be summed up in one word—death. His dream dies, and with Susana, his love. His offspring die, and he kills Comala. So powerful that he controls the lives of all around him, he cannot make death have meaning, not even through love.

> He had thought he knew and understood her. But even if he didn't, wasn't it enough to know that she was the creature he loved best in all the world? And to know also, and this was the most important, that she would help him depart from this world illuminated by the image that erased all other memories?

That redeeming image proved inaccessible to Pedro Páramo, because there is no such image within the tragic vision of Juan Rulfo.

The forces which drive the character Pedro Páramo are independent of any social environment, transcending it. The rhythm of his life story does not correspond to conditions outside Comala, barely alluded to in historical references, for the clues to his behavior lie in more basic human traits. His brutality is made sharper by the startling beauty of his love, the very force of which, converted into hate, determines the depth of his vengeance against Comala, the degree to which the village will be submerged into a timeless inferno.

In contrast to Pedro, and serving as his foil, is the unattainable Susana. Despite their opposition, they have much in common, for both are obsessed with lyrical reveries of past love; "the impregnable fortress of [their] interior dream and pain." In Susana's case, we know nothing of the object of her distress other than sensual musings, for the crisis in her life occurs outside the novel. We can judge that her love was as unattainable as Pedro's from such fragments as these: ". . . but he felt lonely, even though I was there with him." and, a few lines later:

> " 'I like to bathe in the sea,' I told him.
> "But he didn't understand.
> "And the next morning I was out on the beach again, to clean myself. To give myself up to the sea . . . ."

The polarity between Pedro Páramo and Susana is shown by the ways they react to their misery. Pedro responds with violence; Susana retreats to the private hell (and joy) of madness. She becomes completely passive, while his energies burst outward against others. Susana rejects Pedro Páramo and the comfort that religion offers, while he adds the burden of her suffering on to his own. The two counterbalance each other, although Susana is scarcely more than a charcoal sketch.

The lack of conventional character development in *Pedro Páramo* is striking when compared with *The Edge of the Storm.* There is no physical description in the former, for example, while every detail of Don Dionisio's appearance was carefully described, every nuance of his observable actions ferreted out. All this wealth of description helped convince us of his authenticity. With knowledge of his reflections, the reader moved with him as he tried to resolve unreconcilable conflicts. Yáñez showed the changing process of character as well. Don Dionisio learned from experience, and his responses varied depending on the nature of the other characters. He worked quite differently with Father Reyes than with Father Islas, for example. He was also fitted into a sharply focused background, which in turn bestowed upon him greater coherence. In short, he was human, a flesh and blood figure in a real setting.

Juan Rulfo's protagonist is all bony structure and spirit. He is an abstraction, not a human being. Instead of explicit descriptions there are story fragments and scraps of conversation, and most of these issue from illusory sources. Although the novel encompasses the same years, exterior events are of minor importance, and his Jalisco village has little resemblance to the one described by Yáñez. We are dealing now with magic.

Mythic Underpinnings

A key aspect of Rulfo's creation is the aura of myth which invades it. Carlos Fuentes noted this quality in a recent statement: "Juan Rulfo [proceeded] to the mythification of the situations, the character types and the language of rural Mexico. . . ."[11] Fuentes went on to discover links with Greek mythology, finding correspondences between Juan Preciado's search and the Odyssey, between

Dolores Preciado and both Jocasta and Eurydice, mother and lover—suggesting that Juan Preciado embodies elements of the myths of both Oedipus and Orpheus.

Actually, a better case can be made for Fuentes' sharp perception by observing the *quality* of myth than by following vague suggestions of specific Greek tales. For within most cultures, including that of rural Mexico, are motifs of search, of an underworld, of love unrealized. As a whole, Rulfo's novel has the flavor of myth, combining the elements of many. There is the timelessness, the lack of a beginning or an end, and the negation of history, which leaves the legend suspended. Poetic images suggest symbols for the reader who wishes to search for them. Most pertinent of all, the tale is removed from the reality the reader knows to a supernatural realm where life and death have no boundaries.

Pedro Páramo's mythic aura flows organically from its source. Here a clear distinction must be made, eliminating the term "folkloric," with its literary connotations calling to mind descriptions of indigenous or regional customs and idiosyncrasies. The stress in Rulfo falls rather on folk motifs endowed with vast symbolic reference, broad enough to approach universality.

The very substance of *Pedro Páramo* is fashioned from the concept, current in the folk belief of rural Mexico, of "ánimas en pena"—souls in pain, condemned to roam the earth, separated from their corporeal origins. The suggestion is that Eduviges, who we later learn has long since committed suicide, is in this state of being when she serves as the vehicle by which Juan is first introduced to the present and the past of Comala. One of the few "live" persons Juan encounters tells him: ". . . the village is full of spirits, a whole throng of wandering souls that died in sin and can't find any way of getting pardon. . . ." Indeed, one of the spirits whom Juan briefly meets, Damiana, says to him: "Poor Eduviges. Then she must still be suffering."

By contrast, in the second half of the novel, it is in dialogue with the soulless body of Dorotea that Juan completes the process of bringing to light the final phases of Pedro Páramo's life. In a moving answer which establishes in her the same sense of guilt which envelops every character of whom Juan has learned, she tells him of the separation of body and soul:

> "And your soul? Where do you think it's gone?"
>
> "It must be wandering around up there on earth, like all those others, looking for people to pray for it. I think it hates me for the bad things I did, but that doesn't worry me any more. I'm rid of all the pain it used to give me. It made me feel bitter about everything . . . and it made the nights unbearable, full of terrifying thoughts . . . . When I sat down to die, it told me to get up again and keep on living, as if it still hoped for some miracle that would clean away my sins. But I wouldn't. This is the end, I told it. . . I opened my mouth so it could leave, and it left. I felt something fall into my hands. It was the little thread of blood that had tied it to my heart."

Such folk beliefs are so much a part of the structure and so important to Rulfo's assumptions concerning existence that they constitute the living reality of *Pedro Páramo*, superimposing magical elements on the "realistic" narrative process. In this sense, the unearthly Comala falls within the bounds of myth as defined by Richard Chase:

> Literature becomes mythical by suffusing the natural with preternatural force toward certain ends, by cap-

turing the impersonal forces of the world and directing
them toward the fulfillment of certain needs.[12]

*   *   *   *   *

Myth performs the cathartic function of dramatizing
the clashes and harmonies of life in a social and natural
environment. But myth can be understood as the
aesthetic leaven which heals or makes tolerable those
deep neurotic disturbances which in primitive culture
are occasioned by the clashing attitudes of magic and
religion.[13]

The dramatizing of "ánimas en pena" underlies the
device by which a major section of the story is conveyed to
the reader, rendering the narrative perspective of death
authentic. It is made more complex by a third state of being,
also a common folk motif, the animated corpse. Dorotea,
in the passage quoted above, lying in the grave and, at
last, free of the soul that hates her, says, "Heaven is right
here where I am." Susana's corpse is not as satisfied. Her
body continues to writhe as it did in life, until the coffin
breaks.

A number of sub-motifs reinforce the pattern of super-
imposed folk-fantastic elements. In each case they contribute
to the elaboration of a central theme—the blurring of the
lines between life and death, with a resultant fusing of the
two states. On several occasions there are passing, casual
references to communication between living and dead as a
normal pattern, references which fill out the context of Juan
Preciado's initially strange and mysterious encounters.[14]

Other such magical elements are the dead horse which
gallops at night in search of its dead master; the room in
Eduviges' hostelry in which the screams of a hanged man
continue to resound years later; the assumption that Bar-

tolomé appeared after his murder in the form of a cat, to visit his daughter Susana.

On one level, all the above occurrences defy logic and confound rational explanation. On another, they exemplify the supernatural system of belief which, for the rural folk of Mexico, is necessary in order to reconcile otherwise insoluble phenomena. The novel's oscillation between what for the reader are reality and irreality is consonant with the mentality of its characters. This matter-of-fact treatment of magical elements enables Rulfo to absorb the myths of rural Mexico into the total picture he paints. To carry Carlos Fuentes' insight to its logical conclusion, Juan Rulfo has used the situations, the character types, and the language of rural Mexico to create the new myth of Pedro Páramo.

WORLD VIEW

Agustín Yáñez, we have seen, manifested confidence in his capacity to integrate individual peculiarities and conflicts into a basically rational novelistic structure. Rulfo, in large measure, refuses omniscience. His disconnected views of events and people, separating interior conflict from exterior action, are part of his denial of responsibility for an objective overview of man in society. He, the author, considers himself imperfect in his grasp of man, so that he must insist on remaining on the same earthly footing as the reader, rather than above and apart. Thus he requires the reader to suffer with him, to participate in the superhuman attempt to render chaos orderly.

For Yáñez, man in the twentieth century is distinct from his ancestors of several centuries' distance. Now he is able to avail himself, in striving for self-knowledge, of the new tools of science and philosophy, and of new approaches to examining history. Man need not deny the intuitive or the irrational in his psyche, but can assume at a minimum his capability to achieve equilibrium with these elements of his nature—at least to understand them and to live with them.

Rulfo, on the other hand, finds no evidence of change, of evolution, or new self-knowledge. The quest for power in Pedro Páramo, and the evil which overshadows his love, are reminiscent of themes in Greek tragedy. To choose another point of reference, Hugo Rodríguez-Alcalá finds points of contact between the suffering existence of Comala and the Inferno of Dante.

Rulfo's is basically a fatalistic view of existence. The novel's structure, piecing together the shards of an already preordained tragedy, dramatizes Rulfo's cosmic pessimism with regard to man's ability to control his own fortunes, to master himself, to achieve love, or to evolve a meaningful morality. Existence, in these terms, is a closed system, cyclical in its repetition of past patterns and in its reliving of basic mythic themes. Rulfo clearly demonstrates much more affinity for Jung than for Freud.

Written in post-Revolutionary 1955, *Pedro Páramo* condenses extreme bitterness into its evaluation of the Revolution. Implicitly, it runs directly counter to the widely circulated versions of the past two decades of progress and reforms. The fortunes of Mexican man in the novel show no signs of progressing as the nation evolves. On the contrary, the formation of the protagonist's character antedates the Revolution, remains oblivious to it, and survives it unchanged. Within the novel, the Revolution symbolizes the futility of all history in its ineffectual consequences and its essentially barbaric nature.

Rulfo's tragic vision implies the deep inadequacy of Christianity. The weight of a burden closely akin to original sin oppresses not only Pedro Páramo, but Padre Rentería, Susana, and all the minor characters except the neutral observer Juan. But, in opposition to Christian concepts, Rulfo's characters carry this burden through life with no prospect for relief, no effective sacraments to act as countervailing forces, and no hope for redemption in another world, since life and death constitute a continuum. Heaven is beyond the reach of all. Neither religious faith nor humanistic solidarity offer any antidote to a mode of being in which man is condemned to suffer and to cause others to suffer.

There could be no more pitiful a creature than Dorotea, who tries to explain her frustrated maternal instincts in terms of sin-ridden dreams. The lyricism of Pedro's deep longing for Susana is movingly beautiful, as are the memories of Dolores Preciado of a formerly blissful pastoral life in Comala. Yet in each case, an instinct for love and an awareness of beauty are inevitably ground down by the abrasive effects of sin and guilt in the characters themselves, as well as in their fellow men. Susana's question, "And what do you think life is, if not sin?" underlies the entire conceptual fabric of the novel.

In these terms, Rulfo's world contrasts sharply with that of Yáñez, whose anticlericalism implied the need for reform, for new adjustments of moral norms. Rulfo projects doubts so deep as to question any foundations of belief of modern society. On an earth where life has the characteristics of hell, and beauty in effect serves as a gauge of suffering, man's fate is abject and final.

This contrast in world views in Rulfo and Yáñez also relates to the question of the authors' implied attitudes concerning the function of literature. Yáñez, as we have seen, seeks to *realize* his world, incorporating subjective elements —sounds, fears, desires, musical responses, esthetic reactions—into a total structure which has meaning because it can be viewed, even in its complexities and contradictions, against a framework of reason and humanism. For him, the novel is an artistic form for seeking useful truth in the world about him. His reconstruction of the past in elaborate, neo-baroque prose, assumes a close relationship between the esthetic expressiveness of the novel and the light which literature can provide in the search for answers to contemporary dilemmas.

Rulfo proceeds to disintegrate his universe—then he puts together enough pieces to form a coherent, highly personalized expression of despair. His image is magic, poetic, irrational. The novel for him is a means of expressing, in original terms, his own subjectivity. Literature becomes, in Rulfo's sense, a highly individualized art form, and the responsibility of the creative artist is to affix his own distinct seal upon the world, in an act of creation which may well be his only recourse.

CARLOS FUENTES is the only Mexican writer today who is able to live solely by writing. In recent years, which he has spent in Paris, and in the years before that in Mexico City, he has known the luxury and the discipline of daily spending five to six hours at his desk. The results of this routine have been a steady flow of prose fiction, essays on cultural and political themes, and various film scripts.

Fuentes has to his credit two volumes of short stories, *Los días enmascarados* (1954) and *Cantar de ciegos* (1964). Since the appearance of his first novel, *La región más transparente*, in 1958, he has been on center stage of the Mexican literary scene, with his creative works and public positions on literature and politics provoking widespread discussions among intellectual and university circles. Subsequent novels have been *Las buenas conciencias* (1959), *La muerte de Artemio Cruz* (1962), *Aura* (1962), and *Zona sagrada* (1967). *Cambio de piel*, recently published in Spanish and English editions, was the winner in 1967 of an important literary prize in Spain, although the Spanish government has since prohibited its publication there. The English edition is entitled *Change of Skin*. Fuentes is rapidly becoming an international literary figure—his two major novels, *La región más transparente* and *La muerte de Artemio Cruz* have been translated and published in twelve different languages.

In 1966, Fuentes attended the P.E.N. Congress in New York, and subsequently published an article in *Life en Español* which spoke of the Congress as a thaw in the cultural cold war. For this, Fuentes was the recipient of considerable criticism in Havana. He has since reiterated his support of Cuba, and signed a declaration of Latin American writers, published in Havana. The statement affirms the dual task of the writer: to participate as an intellectual in the struggle for basic change in Latin America, and as an artist to remain responsible to his art by whatever techniques and approaches to reality which will serve his creative aims.

Born in Mexico City in 1928, Fuentes spent his youth abroad in many Western capitals, as his father moved from one diplomatic post to another. He has vivid memories of Washington, D.C., Santiago, Buenos Aires, and Rio de Janeiro. His education includes a law degree from the National University of Mexico and advanced studies in international relations in Geneva.

Since 1955, when he was cofounder with Emmanuel Carballo of the *Revista Mexicana de Literatura,* Fuentes has been outspoken on the major intellectual issues of the day. Taken together, his public positions fill out the profile of an independent figure of the Mexican and Latin American left. He has been critical of the Soviet Union's treatment of Russian writers, and of the tenets of "socialist realism," yet he was also an early supporter of the Cuban Revolution and Fidel Castro, and did not hesitate to condemn United States intervention in the Dominican Republic. In 1962, he incurred the wrath of the State Department, which denied him a visa, thus preventing his appearance on an NBC television program. Fuentes had been scheduled to take the opposing side in a debate on the Alliance for Progress, the defender to be Richard Goodwin, President Kennedy's special adviser on Latin American affairs.

4 | THE QUEST FOR IDENTITY: CARLOS FUENTES

Where the Air is Clear
(La región más transparente)

WITH THE EMERGENCE of Carlos Fuentes as Mexico's most dynamic young writer,[1] the central locale of the novel becomes Mexico City, the nation's capital and nerve center. Here in a bursting metropolis reflecting simultaneously the sweep of 400 years of history and the dynamics of the neo-capitalist period of the post-Revolution, a new generation of highly educated intellectuals, some fifteen years younger than Rulfo and twenty-five years younger than Yáñez, in the early 1950's undertook the task of challenging the myths handed down to them by their fathers, the makers of the Revolution.

Stimulated by the philosopher Leopoldo Zea and by the poet-essayist Octavio Paz, they refused to accept the gospel of nationalism, insisting upon conducting their own examination of the status of Mexico and the Mexicans in the light of universal ideas such as existentialism, and in the mood of post-World War II thought the world over, with its shadings of doubt, individualism, and disillusionment. The result was a prolific outpouring of essays and books analyzing the Mexican character, Mexican psychology, the shortcomings of the Revolution, and the limitations imposed on art and literature by a formerly constructive climate of nationalism. It was in this charged atmosphere, in which he participated enthusiastically, that Carlos Fuentes began a remarkable career in the novel.

Where the Air is Clear[2] represents Fuentes' first assault on the mountain—a dynamic ascent toward a summit so lofty as to be obscured by clouds. In this first novel, Fuentes mustered all the vitality of the new age in a burst of innovation and a heady effusion of prose. Despite the clouds, he produced a personal document of artistic merit, an intuitive synthesis of the historical emergence of modern Mexico, and a valiant attempt at identifying the spiritual constants unique to the national psyche. In retrospect, given the time, the place, and the ideological circumstances, it was a novel that now appears to have been almost inevitable.

The essentials of Fuentes' first novel cannot be communicated by means of a traditional plot summary, with an attempt to integrate characters and setting. In the final analysis, the novel is a multilayered view of Mexico City, itself a symbol for the new nation. A number of characters participate and interact, but the end product depends as much on style and structure as on the specific resolution of the characters' destinies. Thematic depth develops from

what the characters represent, their contrasting problems
and viewpoints.

The most accessible point of entry, however, is through
the people whose lives are woven into the narrative. In
effect, there is no central protagonist. Like Federico Robles
and Rodrigo Pola, two of the more interesting, most of the
characters are more significant as prototypes than memorable as individuals.

Robles, a child of the Revolution, from a poor Indian
family in Michoacán, rises through a series of accidental
circumstances, on which his aggressiveness enables him to
capitalize, to a position of wealth and influence. With the
persuasive forcefulness of present-day captains of Mexican
society (the novel is set early in the 1950's), he advocates
the development of an upper-middle class of domestic cap-
italists in order to consolidate permanently the gains of the
Revolution. It is this logic which rationalizes self-enrichment in a morass of clandestine financial transactions and
real-estate dealings. Robles has married a beautiful social
climber, Norma, in order to reinforce his economic power
with social status, and a frigid pattern of marriage is offset by his deeply passionate emotional ties to his blind
mistress. The mistress, Hortensia, epitomizes the qualities
of female suffering and stoicism. Having been brutalized by
a spinelessly bellicose husband in a tragic earlier marriage,
she now is able to concentrate her entire being and her
capacity for love into her moments with Robles, in which
both give generously of themselves. The dimensions of this
love provide a clue to the other side of Robles' driving personality, for which Hortensia is the wellspring of stability.

Robles' power is finally broken by rebels who band
together in corrupt manipulation of both finances and public
opinion. A bitter confrontation with his wife explodes in

anger, resulting in a fire which symbolically consummates Norma's death. When last heard of, in an indirect reference, Robles has left for northern Mexico with Hortensia, whom he has married, and has begun a new existence in modern cotton farming.

A number of literary factors prevent Robles' career from emerging as merely a meteoric and melodramatic saga which reproduces in urban terms the narrative simplicity of a novel of the Revolution. Foremost is this novel's collage structure, juxtaposing nonsequential fragments in apparently illogical order. Successive chapters, skipping back and forth from the present to various points in the past, highlight at one moment scenes of action in Mexico City and, at the next, detailed remembrances of one or another character's early life. A wide variety of brief sections are also interspersed. For example, evocative prose odes initiate and end the novel, introducing symbols of life in Mexico City. Other sections, in different narrative tones, ranging from camera documentary to suggestive parable, insert vignettes which capture fleeting glimpses of life among the city's anonymous masses and classes. The threads of Robles' life must be picked out and reintegrated by the reader.

A second factor is the weight of the past. Third-person flashbacks or accounts by other characters fill in the formative periods in Robles' story—his childhood when the early stirrings of the Revolution reached his humble family, his adolescence under a priest's tutelage and a first experience of instinctual love for the latter's niece, his career as a general's aide in revolutionary campaigns, his training in law and subsequent rise to power. Beneath the corrupt exterior, Robles has a conscience with roots in the revolutionary years. It is this ambiguity which identifies his dilemma with Mexico's agonizing leap into the twentieth century.

Similarly, Rodrigo Pola is a character whose development in large part consists of a struggle to reject the containing restrictions imposed by an overly protective mother —herself another variant of the suffering female. Having lost her husband in the Revolution, she follows a pattern which combines continual reliving of the past with an impossible concentration on her son. It is a process which attempts to keep him a dependent entity, as though in a state of constantly emerging from the womb, and simultaneously to install him as the dominant male figure in her life.

Rodrigo's fate has an ironic cast. The career of his father, which weighed heavily on his own, had been a moral failure. The elder Pola had left a young pregnant wife in order to fight for ideals in the Revolution, only to die a humiliating death after betraying his comrades in arms so that he would not have to face a firing squad alone.

Rodrigo's adolescent resistance to maternal domination takes the form, in the 1920's, of sincere aspirations to write poetry and a timid love for the young Norma who later married Robles. After his mother's death he is finally able to find social stability and to achieve an apparent confidence in himself, although he never recovers from Norma's scornful rejection. His situation at the novel's end constitutes an ironic return to the empty pre-Revolutionary values of the mother he had deserted in the days before her death. He has become a morally corrupt screenwriter, his early love for poetry now grotesquely transformed into scenarios of a crass neobourgeois variety, pandering to the lowest common denominator of public taste. His newfound status is confirmed and enhanced by marriage to Pimpinela de Ovando, descendant of an aristocratic family of Porfirian vintage, who is able to trade on the appeal which her name holds for the prestige-conscious *nouveau riche* class produced by the Revolution.

The uneven rhythm of the novel alternates between long scenes detailing the personal history of characters like Robles and Pola, and rapid-fire chapters set in present-day Mexico City. Some of the most dynamic sections are those capturing the decadent social whirl of the Pola-Robles upper-middle class—the cocktail parties, the myriad forms of furious competition for social status. Here the author wields a deft brush, sketching with suggestive dialogue the wit, the aggressiveness, the false veneer of sophistication of this parasitic world. In this social orbit, populated by bankers, pseudo-intellectuals, minor European royalty, mistresses, and journalists, the values which stand out are cynicism, profound respect for economic and political power, intellectual snobbery, contempt for all thing Mexican, and nostalgia for the aura and the artifacts of the Porfirio Díaz era.

Superimposed on all the important action is the ambiguous figure of Ixca Cienfuegos, who is literally both character and symbol. Never completely real, his physical appearance is always communicated in abstract terms ("Cienfuego's paralyzed smile was denied by his dense and obscure eyes, narrowed in a gaze of hatred . . . .") His existence in the novel seems guided by some higher, magical purpose, endowing him with an omniscience which permits him to enter the life of each character.

Yet his role is not merely that of witness-conscience, engaging in dialogue and raising challenging questions which, in Rodrigo's case, force him to take cognizance of the real meaning of his life from beginning to end. At other moments, Ixca participates actively, with devastating purposefulness, in the turn of events. Thus he sets in motion, via Pimpinela, the rumors concerning Robles which ultimately bring about the latter's downfall. Further, perceiving the vulnerability of Norma, he relentlessly and coldly seduces her in an effort to impel her destruction—a goal which is ultimately achieved in the flames of Robles' burning house.

Ixca is not only the incarnation of the monstrous metropolis in all its dynamism, its suffering, its blemished humanity. He also incarnates the values and myths of Indian Mexico, in particular the timeless sense of betrayal and the compulsion to reestablish ties with the past by means of sacrifice.

Thus, *Where the Air is Clear* relives, through figures such as Robles, the historic sweep of the Revolution and the dramatic changes wrought by this popular upsurge, just as in Ixca it simultaneouly asserts the presence of the Indian world view, Mexico's cultural subsoil, rich in myths and symbols.

STRUCTURE

In mounting his narrative collage, Fuentes continued and extended the tendency, evident in Yáñez and important in Rulfo, toward a nonchronological sequence of events.

Chapters and even parts of chapters are juxtaposed in accordance with thematic needs rather than adhering to temporal sequence. The author shows more concern for amplifying the novel's scope horizontally—in the world of Mexico City—and vertically—back in time to include individual and historical past—than for developing a story-centered plot.

This fragmented structure performs a variety of literary functions. In the first place, it brings the weight of the past to bear on the present at judicious moments and in a selective manner. Thus after the prologue and two initial chapters introducing the cast of characters and the contextual themes of Mexico City, five chapters round out the novel's first part. Their titles, respectively, are "Gervasio Pola (1919)," "Los de Ovando (1910-1951)," "Federico Robles (1907-1951)," "Norma Larragoiti (1920-1940)," and "Rodrigo Pola (1914-1932)." Varying in narrative form and point of view, each projects backward to key moments or periods in the earlier life of an individual character. At the same time, each chapter is linked to the present in different ways: by connection to the present thought process of an individual figure, by being part of the recollections which various individuals offer to Ixca, or by being bounded on both sides by fragments of present-time narration, so that past experiences form a living part of the consciousness, thought and outlook of the characters as they confront present-day problems. Further, in each chapter, narrative links establish connections with other characters already introduced in the novel. For example, the chapter on Robles' youth crosses paths with the families of Rodrigo Pola, Pimpinela de Ovando, and the intellectual, Manuel Zamacona.

A second service which the consciousness of time performs for Fuentes is to enable him to compare and contrast the subjective and objective dimensions of reality. For Robles and Pola, the novel's sudden backward leaps serve to highlight determinant experiences in youth, crises and climaxes whose formative effects molded personality and influenced later decisions. These individuals are shaped by crucial moments in their lives, which are more important to their personalities than steady development and maturation across time. Yet they simultaneously react to the flow of historical events in the world around them, particularly to the unfolding of the Revolution.

An example, from Robles' point of view, of the sharp contrast between subjective and objective reality is evident in his thoughts on the two women in his life. Relations with Norma, geared to his exterior life, to his role in society, are rational and predictable. Hortensia is the key to his deeply personal subjective existence, unpredictable in its peaks and valleys. The contrast is measured by concepts of time:

> Robles tried to intuit this, the difference between the two women. To go to bed with Norma was not dangerous. With Hortensia, only with Hortensia, to make love was a somersault in air; you never knew what veil would be torn or what fire-glass would burn your tongue, what support beneath either life, his or hers, would be destroyed or created when the moment ended. Norma's ceremony was always as precise as the four corners of a watch dial. And Hortensia was time itself, unmeasured hours. Untouchable and silent, she demanded an answer without words . . . held and nourished her entire life, awaiting the moment when she would loosen the controls and exhaust all the blood accumulated across limitless time in two, in four limited minutes.

In an analogous embodiment of this dual view of time and reality, the novel's structure itself is a constant, often bewildering juxtaposition of narrative pieces, switching abruptly from action to thought, from outside to inside, from an objective view of circumstances to a subjective interpretation of these circumstances.

A third effect is simultaneity in the present. By contrast with the narrative sweeps into the past, which seem chaotic in their movements, the treatment of the horizontal dimensions is carefully insistent on capturing events and emotions at precisely the same moment in time. Thus all the diverse personal backgrounds and the multitude of causal effects from Mexican history are channeled into the actions of characters whom we see, at various points in the novel, acting out their lives simultaneously, as though on separate but adjacent stages.

One such point comes within the second chapter, thirty-five pages of which have an ultrasophisticated party for a narrative framework. Much in the manner of the party sequence in Aldous Huxley's *Point Counter Point,* the fourteen scenes or sections which make up these pages dart back and forth, introducing characters in rapid dialogue scenes which communicate a preliminary impression of their personalities, usually with mordant underlying irony. In seven of these sections, the narrative camera swings out of range of the party itself, to relate incidents occurring, or thoughts being thought elsewhere. Twice in such sections there are references to the party, setting up direct links. The rapidity of the scenes, the sharpness of the dialogue, and the deft, contrapuntal play of characters combine to introduce the major cast of the novel in terms of their spoken words and their interior thoughts as they come together, cross paths, and separate before our eyes. Only later does the narrative focus become differential, swinging back to the past to illuminate the antecedents of these intensely concentrated personal relationships which bring together in relatively few pages a wide variety of characters.

Within the party itself, certain scenes are skilfully interlinked in time, so that various characters and dialogues are frozen at one precise moment. An example is found when a vacuous discussion among a group of intellectuals on the significance of poetry ends with the statement in French, "Certainly, love is a reality in the realm of imagination." There follows a scene outside the party among secondary characters whose connections with the main threads of the novel will become apparent only later. In the next section, Rodrigo Pola approaches the group of intellectuals just in time to hear the sentence, "Certainly, love is a reality in the realm of the imagination." Not only are the moments pulled together, but the intervening action, we now realize, has been simultaneous.

A similar chapter toward the novel's end, within the framework of Mexican independence celebrations on September 15, provides an element of structural balance, matching the early scenes of the party chapter. Once more, within the imposed simultaneity of an explosive fiesta, a number of short sections extend the coverage to diverse characters. Whereas the earlier chapter had been introductory, now the narrative aim is crystallization. Many individual destinies take definitive shape here. In fact, three secondary figures meet highly significant deaths—Norma, Gabriel, and Jorgito. Again, counterpoint comes into play, as Rodrigo and Robles move in opposing directions. The former definitively assumes the mask of hypocrisy, while the latter approaches the final casting off of his role as captain of modern Mexican finance.

The balance between these two chapters, themselves internally similar, each illuminating the complexities of multiple characters, provides a measure of coherence for an overall structure which seems put together at random. In general, the technique of simultaneity in *Where the Air is Clear* heightens the immediacy of the present.

Ixca Cienfuegos, half real, half spirit, partly witness, partly active character, constitutes a structural element in the novel. A shadowy figure whose strange aura of cold forcefulness commands entrée to all, he is able to interview Robles, Pola, and many others. One character says of him, "Like God; he's everywhere, but no one ever sees him. In and out of government offices, society drawing rooms, friend of magnates. They say he's the brain behind some banker, or that he's a gigolo or just a marijuana addict. He comes, he goes . . . ."

Ixca's drive to revive a consciousness of ties with Mexico's pre-Hispanic culture roots colors his relationships with other characters, so that he channels dialogue toward the past, evoking from them memories and half-forgotten accounts which serve to identify the keys to each personality. In his search for a victim whose death will constitute the equivalent of traditional sacrifice, Ixca functions both as a link between characters and a vehicle for narrative probing of the past. His probing infuses myth and irreality into a work which otherwise might have been a realistic novel of social criticism.

A final structural component is almost direct borrowing of the "Camera Eye" used by John Dos Passos in *U.S.A.*, as Samuel O'Neill has pointed out.[3] Eleven of the chapters in the second part of *Where the Air is Clear* are preceded by unrelated vignettes entitled, as in Dos Passos, by the first words of the particular text. Continuing the pattern of constantly changing narrative focus, they serve primarily to fill out the panoramic context of Mexico City— its raw, smelly marketplaces, its corrupt precinct courthouses—and to provide glimpses of its inhabitants and their values—the newly arrived artisan from the provinces, aspiring to begin a small business; the lower-middle-class husband harried by a woefully empty young wife with dreams of automobiles and a little cottage; the old man mourning the stability of the *porfiriato,* gone forever from a city "ruined" by the Revolution; the bored prostitute routinely downing an evening meal before beginning her evening shift.

Two of the vignettes are different in tone. One provides a glimpse back in time as Ixca surveys the city from Robles' skyscraper office, summoning forth other eras when heroes had prevailed. Anticipating the final prose ode to Mexico City, it is a compressed vision of a surface metropolis atop a many-layered historic sediment, with the intangible presence of the Conquest, the Reform, and the Revolution still felt.

Another piece, almost a parable of two ragged men eking out an existence from their performing dog, is strongly reminiscent of the prose fiction of Juan José Arreola in its tone of distilled sadness for the human condition. Brief though they are, these vignettes serve to flesh out the drama and the unresolved tensions of Mexico City, accentuating its role as an active, dynamic environment in the novel, rather than merely the background against which the characters act out their individual dramas. Echoes of many of them reappear in the synthesizing conclusion.

Despite the range of substantive matter and thematic connotations opened up by the unorthodox structure of *Where the Air is Clear,* the novel suffers, on the whole, from formlessness. Notwithstanding intricate relationships between characters, extending into the past and piecing together a partial plot framework, the three major parts do not stand in a clear enough relationship to each other. Further, two of them are weighted down by overly long flashbacks. In particular, those of Rosenda, the mother of Rodrigo, and Mercedes, the first love of Robles and mother of his illegitimate son Manuel Zamacona, tend to be tedious in the wealth of detail and analysis which they provide concerning secondary characters.

In addition, the key character, Ixca Cienfuegos, on whom structure depends, is imprecise. He hovers precariously between reality and fantastic symbolism, partaking of both modes of existence and therefore never quite blending into the novelistic fabric. Samuel O'Neill points out, "As a character himself, he is not well handled psychologically. He is a cold unbelievable personality. There is little justification for his wanderings and no causal relationship between him and the self-revelation of the characters."[4] Actually, there is something of an explanation, but it does not stem inherently from the narration. At the novel's end, when it is too late to undo the underlying confusion, the reader perceives that the personality of Ixca rests on two bases. On the one hand, he is controlled by his mother Teódula, a semi-mythic figure herself, who impels him to find in modern Mexico ties to the Aztec past. Further, as the final ode metaphorically suggests, Ixca somehow embodies the conscience and the consciousness of Mexico City. But this is an explanation radically different in causal pattern from that of the other characters, and its vagueness weakens novelistic structure.

Notwithstanding its shortcomings, the open structure makes possible a highly original penetration into the past and present complexities, which underlie contemporary Mexico.

MODES OF NARRATION

Where the Air is Clear, by comparison with *The Edge of the Storm* and *Pedro Páramo,* is considerably more complex in modes of narration, in stylistic development, and in conscious assimilation of influences from European and American literature. Many of the techniques employed, already familiar in other literature, were new to Mexico—especially such a large number of innovations within the covers of one novel.

In keeping with the collage pattern of structure, the forms in which narration is presented to the reader are changing and disparate. The ambiental world acquires a personality of its own because it is revealed at times independently of direct relationship to the several plot lines. This independence stems from the narrative approximation of the cinematic camera, partly a Dos Passos technique, partly due no doubt to Fuentes' personal experiences in the film industry.

Thus, the vignettes mentioned above are usually anecdotal fragments from daily life, documenting snatches of conversation or momentary glimpses of problems whose representative qualities impart the flavor of city life.

In addition to the roving camera, there are other instances of cinematic borrowing. On the day after the long party scene of the second chapter, the narrative equivalent of an introductory "pan shot" is employed to survey the morning atmosphere, zooming in to focus on one after another of the key characters whose backgrounds will subsequently be developed in individual chapters:

> Eleven in the morning. Cars roared by on Insurgentes, on Niza, where mansions from Porfirio Díaz days began the decline toward boutiques, restaurants, beauty shops. The sun beat down. No breeze stirred Reforma's

graceful tree crowns. Federico Robles stared down over the unsteady urban pastiche from the ninth floor of a rose stone building . . . . Vaporous glass facades showed him their backsides of painted brick and beer ads. In the distance, at the foot of the mountains, a whirlwind of dust collected its brown atoms. Here, close, the racket of laborers drilling a street surface. Wreaths of secretaries and paunchy sidewalk vendors and skirt-watchers wove among strands of beggars and elderly gringos who told stories about Peoria. Glancing at their watches, bald men dressed in grey ran by, tattered briefcases in hand.

One more, one more, signaled the fingers of cabdrivers. Cars raced, zigzagging, squeezed together, tántaranta-tán-tán. Their horns woke Rodrigo Pola; the city's shameless noises filtered through cracks into his inside room on Rosales Street. On the roof of her home surrounded by Chapultepec Hills, Norma Larragoiti de Robles spread out cushions and took off her silk wrapper . . . and annointed her body. Sun tan. Hortensia Chacón, forever in darkness, waited for sounds from Tonalá Street, waited for afternoon school to let out, and for the sound of a key in the lock. Avenida Mixcoac wended its way, presided over by vegetable stores, variety shops and third-rate movies, to the sound of steamrollers, picks and air-hammers; but none of that reached the sealed room where Rosenda Pola slept, as always in delirious slumber . . . Charlotte, Pierrot, Silvia Régules, Gus, Prince Vampa, Pichi, Junior, all were sleeping. Only Pimpinela de Ovando was ready for the new day, straight and perfumed, behind dark glasses, walking down Madero to Roberto Régules' office. Before Robles' eyes,

> Mexico City fanned out like a deck of playing cards
> . . . the ace of spades at Santo Domingo, the three
> of hearts at Polanco. . . .

That Fuentes was strongly conscious of the cinema is
evident not only in his borrowings of techniques, but in his
thematic treatment of the Mexican film industry as the
epitome of the commercialization of artistic values—the
moral snake pit into which Rodrigo Pola descends in his
flight from consciousness of self. Further, he makes reference on occasion to film classics as a source of comparison
to the behavior of his characters. Rodrigo, in a sentimental
conversation with Natasha, is suddenly reminded of a scene
from *The Blue Angel,* with the roles inverted—Natasha
playing a feminine Emil Jannings to his own masculine
Marlene Dietrich. Natasha even sings a few lines of "Sura-
baya Johnny."

Cinematic techniques and themes impart a modernity
to the novel, even though such techniques were already
growing stale in the United States. They reflect the modernity of neocapitalist Mexico.

Another technique for communicating environmental
background, again inspired by Dos Passos and foreshad-
owed in *The Edge of the Storm,* is the narrative pastiche of
historical fragments, newspaper headlines, advertisements,
social commentary, and popular songs, all dizzyingly inter-
mixed. An example is the sequence of memories which flash
into the mind of Robles as he tells Ixca of a moment in his
past, when President Obregón began to channel the nation's
attention from the battlefield to the arena of reform and
stabilization:

> Robles' eyes were narrowed to slits. "The nation
> was destroyed. Ten years of disorder, no plans, nearly

a million dead. The General realized how things stood, and in 1920, after Carranza's death, he disbanded his troops . . . ."
"I DO NOT SEEK THE PRESIDENCY," SAYS DE LA HUERTA
VILLA MURDERED
Pancho Villa is dead,
They murdered him from ambush,
Poor old Pancho Villa,
You'll find him now in the graveyard.
But not he, he moved straight toward what he saw coming: business.

> the spot which will remain the center of style and wealth
> in the capital: the "Don Quijote" cabaret of the Hotel Regis

he knew that pretorianism was coming to an end in Mexico
ESTRADA'S TROOPS HAVE TAKEN GUADALA-JARA
that it had seen its high noon in the Revolution, and that if Mexico wanted to progress, it had to permit the bourgeois seeds, incubating since the Reform, to sprout.[5]

The passage attempts to approximate mental recall, showing how Robles reconstructs the flavor of the dynamic tensions which then prevailed.

Not only environment but also characterization and, above all, dialogue are illuminated by language. One of the strengths of the novel is a sensitivity to shadings of meaning and values in everyday language. This sensitivity comes across best in dialogue.

Two contrasting examples are the various party and cocktail scenes of the bohemian upper crust, and the family and social life of Gabriel, an urban worker who has tasted the adventure of *bracero* existence in Texas and California. The language of the smart set, sharp and allusive, is replete with Gallicisms and American sophistication, with literary namedropping, with avid gossip on sexual matters, and an insistence on cleverness. Among Gabriel and his associates, language is harsh and direct, expressing the abrasiveness of daily social relationships, a mixture of extreme aggressiveness with moments of sentimentalism and genuine fraternal emotion. Especially notable is their interpolation of crude English into ordinary speech patterns, connoting the harsh unpleasantness of *bracero* life. Apart from the shock value of the profanity, it reveals the contamination of a vulnerable set of cultural values by many offensive features of American culture, just as the speech of the literati undergoes corruption.

Dialogue is sometimes extended to become almost debate. There are several such instances in which the essential action is the interplay of ideas, which help to define the personalities of Ixca, Robles, Rodrigo, and Zamacona, but primarily serve to extend the thematic implications of the novel. Two such debates are the confrontation between Robles and Zamacona—the old guard of the Revolution versus the new —and a three-way discussion between these two characters and Ixca. Both sections, relatively free of descriptive accompaniment, allow attention to focus on the conceptual fireworks, which the reader must then integrate into the fabric of the novel.

At given moments, Fuentes stylizes dialogue to the point of rendering particular scenes in the form of a dramatic script. When Rodrigo's memories veer back to his adolescent group of would-be poets, the mannerisms and affectations of teen-age literati are rendered as a theater scene, complete with stage directions.

Another mode of dialogue takes the form of rapid-fire telephone conversation. The author compresses into an uninterrupted series of six calls by Roberto Régules the dizzy pace and the internal workings of the financial downfall of Robles, as engineered by Régules. Here dialogue, or rather the half which the reader overhears, provides a sense of immediacy.

The narrative methods traditionally used to probe character—interior monologue, indirect analysis, and dialogue— all function in *Where the Air is Clear* to convey ideas and themes rather than personal characteristics.[6] In general, Fuentes subordinates the literary aspects of psychological analysis to a more informative and exemplary purpose. Rather than strive for a Joycean approximation of the vagaries of the mental process, his efforts tend to identify experiences, traits, and thoughts which are more immediately susceptible to broader reference in the world outside the character. His interest lies more with representative qualities than with psychological idiosyncrasies.

Ixca is the central narrative medium for accomplishing this purpose by evoking introspection. He functions not only as witness, but also as conscience, actively seeking to channel individual thoughts toward the collective. At one point in Rodrigo's narration of childhood experiences, the latter extrapolates a personal self-evaluation, which Ixca redirects:

> "You learn who you are from the time you're very young. Afterwards, I knew that I was what I felt myself to be at that moment: a spy. That is, an onlooker, des-

tined to make my life out of others' lives. And that was all. And I realized something worse, my ability to understand all my defects, and my inability to rise above them."

"You resemble the nation," said Ixca.

A moment later Rodrigo, following Ixca's change in the line of discussion, is saying, "For God's sake, what is this country, Ixca? Where is it going? What can be done with it?" Ixca, then, is a figure quite different from Juan Preciado, the witness-narrator of *Pedro Páramo*, who gathers together the various fragments, largely of exterior events, which recompose the life of Pedro Páramo in an aura of moral abstraction. Ixca's more active role is to piece together fragments of several lives, including their interior dimensions, so that they acquire new meaning in the mixed light of Mexican history, both for the characters and for the reader. In this process of self-knowledge, personal and collective, he is almost a psychoanalyst.

A case in point is Hortensia's lengthy introspections, alternating with brief, guarded, spoken dialogue with Ixca, reviewing a personal history whose ingredients are familiar, but probing into the meanings below the surface. Biographically, her memories rapidly sketch in the stages of her unhappy life up to the point of meeting Robles. The passages are colored by her acceptance of suffering, qualified by an insistence on achieving her own identity as a woman through this very process of suffering:

". . . he has never raised me high, nor dragged me down, but has loved me as I am, with bitter memories, with burned out eyes . . . he gives me his man's love. His love and his hate. Yes, he has taken me away from my children. He pays for their board, but that isn't the same. Maybe that's why I hate him, and I've told him. But that's what he wants, my love and my hate; the first alone would be only half my life . . . . But Federico's brutality is sweet, you know. It's that part of brutality which I want and deserve, as I want and deserve my life, because I know that the true, monstrous brutality he reserves for his dealings with men, for the uses he makes of the people around him . . . . When Federico recognizes that I exist, that at least one person exists outside him, outside what he has been, then he'll become what he should have been. That's the world I have wanted."

This is hardly the untutored Hortensia speaking, but rather Fuentes. Unconvincing as it is as interior monologue, it is nonetheless moving as a verbalization of feelings—what she would say if she could put it into words. The author does not hesitate to give them to her if they help shed light on the main themes and concepts which engross him. Ideas in this case take precedence over the autonomy of character.

This same concern underlies other techniques used in psychological analysis. There are many instances of indirect analysis, in which the author tells us, in third person, what is transpiring in his character's mind. Such an instance occurs when Manuel Zamacona, idealistic intellectual, enters the Robles' garden and notes the faces of beggar women and children through the fence. They await a handout of food scraps and used clothing. His thoughts not only characterize him but touch upon a major thematic thread, the anachronistic, unchanging presence of the Indian throughout Mexican history:

At the end of the garden, behind the fence, a dozen brown faces were squeezed together, some shaded by straw hats, others wrapped to the mouth in *rebozos,* all motionless. Manuel tried to discover some individuality in them, but none revealed more than mute, fixed waiting: closed lips, dark eyes wiped empty of glitter, high cheekbones. Manuel thought of them as identical in all epochs, all ages. Like a subterranean river, indifferent and dark, that flowed below any idea or any change.

The author demonstrates the same purposefulness in handling other narrative forms which approximate inner existence: the subconscious dream of Beto and Gladys, laden with the symbols of a pre-Hispanic creation myth; the personal written notes of Rodrigo and Manuel, more philosophical in tone than indicative of the turn of personality.

In general, Fuentes treats his characters as living embodiments of the multiple thematic crosscurrents which make up Mexican life. As a result, they emerge more as representative types than as unique individuals. Some are more convincing than others. Nonetheless, the complexities which they represent are incorporated into the novelistic whole in a fresh and creative manner by the sophisticated variation of narrative modes.

STYLE

Matching the multifaceted structure of *Where the Air is Clear* is its sweeping range of stylistic tones. One of the bases for Fuentes' modernity is his flexibility with language, which he mines for all it will yield. Although his explorations in this first novel carried him to excess, the work constitutes a stylistic proving ground for the young author.

One contrast which stands out is oscillation between realistic and poetic language. The subproletarian world of

Beto and Gabriel is communicated in earthy terms, explicit in colloquial profanity. The daily frustrations and unpleasantness of their lives are expressed in passages bordering on caricature, aggressively cataloguing its ugliness:

". . . In that cabaret where I waited tables, I had it made. But after a while the old waiters began to snap at you and you feel like shit. . . . They're just washed-up bums. And those slick-talking bastards who come in night after night looking for a fight. No, *mano*. . . . But what else is left? You push an ice-cream cart and it's the same thing. No, *mano*. So what the hell, you go look for a job up north. They give you dollars, you come back home to live it up in your own neighborhood, and no one can screw you. So the gringos treat you like shit? What the hell, that's what they pay you for."

"God damn son of a bitch."

"The bastards! And when they spray that stuff to kill lice all over you, and make you strip, and even cut your hair, you feel like . . ."

"Like grabbing a whip and . . ."

"A whole bunch of poor bastards squeezed into a room like a cattle-stall, everybody naked and smelling like a whorehouse with that . . ."

"D.D.T."

"Yeah, that's it. And a big six-foot gringo hollering 'greaser' at you and snooping through all your stuff. But what the hell, you'll never see the bastard again. . . . And once the harvest is over, they kick you out on your ass. But when you come back over the border, you even remember how pretty that land was. Here it's all desert and dirty Indians."

Totally opposed in tone are the instances in which female characters like Hortensia and Rosenda attempt to express for themselves their emotional problems. Thus Hortensia mentally reconstructs the unhappy relationship with her former husband, seeking through poetic images to evoke the ephemeral and paradoxical meaning of sex:

> "That's what he wanted of women, because he went in search of talk more than sex, because talk he could take away with him and with it he could make an impression in his circles of prestige and praise and confidences, but with sex none of that is possible because it is consumed in a second, between two alone, and that act never again can be recovered—it's too bitter to be recounted for prestige, too small and cruel to impress friends; it disappears and yet it remains inside to cure the deep wound it has caused. . . ."

This passage, which continues in one sentence for an additional page, is typical in its profusion and accumulation of images, of some of the verbose, elaborate qualities of Fuentes' prose, as well as his penchant for speaking through his characters.

A second pattern of stylistic contrast is Fuentes' alternating between the language of the intellect and the language of the senses. The journal of Manuel Zamacona, in which he records his musings on power, moral values, responsibility, and the like, provides a brief, semiphilosophical essay, dealing in abstract concepts. Similarly, various debate scenes largely revolve around intellectual interpretations of Mexican history and politics.

By contrast, a sense-dominated scene is one in which Robles, aroused by a sexual sensation, recalls a similar feeling from the past. The process juxtaposes the experiences of sex and physical combat, and from there his mind skips to unresolved discussions with Ixca and Zamacona, confusing the two. The suggestion is that the discussions have provoked doubts deep in his mind. In this Proustian process, the mind functions at the behest of the senses:

> At the moment of culmination he had taken her hair in his teeth, and his clenched teeth in the darkness had summoned up—fixed in his memory, resuscitated from the chaos of the past few days, extracted from the surrounding elements of his daily life—the image of the battlefield at Celaya, the day when he had bitten the reins of his horse and felt his entire body erect to fight, surrounded by men and the crashing of battle, and his feeling of power in his horse, his erect flesh, the rein he had bitten. Cienfuegos' questions, sharp and clear, returned to his mind. He closed his eyes again— it wasn't Cienfuegos asking the questions in his memory, it was the young man who that afternoon had lunched at his house . . . .

There are numerous ingenious uses of language which incorporate the spirit of modern American and European writers. Samuel O'Neill noted the use of *jitanjáfora* in the frantic party scenes.[7] Afro-Cuban lyrics with their nonsense syllables and rhythmical sounds are interpolated to indicate how the various ultrasophisticated conversations, some of them larded with phrases in English, French, German, Italian, and Latin, are drowned out by the strident cadence of meaningless language and sensual music. Taken together with the corrupted Spanish of the *braceros* and the tourists' English floating in the air in restaurants, the net effect of all these shadings of non-Spanish is to demonstrate via language the tangible presence on the Mexican scene of foreign influences. For all the social levels involved, the use of foreign languages carries an ironic tone, suggesting that the intrusions are negative in character.

The tone of sarcastic irony with which Fuentes views the patterns and mores of upper-class Mexican society serves as an astringent counterbalance to the deeper note of underlying tragedy in the lives of the main characters. Saving this sarcasm from the trap of superficial caricature is the deftness of dialogue, and the fact that several middle-class figures can themselves be devastatingly ironic, indicating a sense of their own hypocrisy. Thus Natasha comments on the Mexican intelligentsia: "And the intellectuals! *Chère, chère,* they are to intelligence what spit is to a letter—a way, *tu sais,* to lick the stamp and make it stick." Similarly, a brief fragment of dialogue from the party, reproduced in its entirety:

"He asks if you're a homosexual, Gus."
"Homo, yes, sexual, who knows."

Perhaps the most original stylistic aspect of *Where the Air is Clear* is its incorporation of the symbols and concepts of pre-Hispanic culture. Occurring most frequently in the thoughts of Ixca Cienfuegos, a flow of metaphoric language based on eagles, serpents, sacrificial knives of obsidian, cycles of the sun and moon, flowers, and mirrors—all presumably key images of the Aztec psyche—stands in contrast to the caustically delineated world of contemporary Mexico City.

Through Ixca, and also in the introductory ode to Mexico City and the final crescendo of the novel's poetic finale, this language serves to rarefy the novelistic atmosphere by enveloping its characters and events in the aura of myth. An overview of Mexico City is seen at moments from the perspective of the Aztec. At one point, for example, Ixca attempts to entice a poor boy into accepting his offer of food. The real aim is apparently to secure a sacrificial victim. The boy intuitively resists, and as he breaks away, bites Ixca's hand. The latter stands contemplating the historic *Zócalo* which is the scene of the action, his thoughts stimulated by his experience and by the taste of his blood as he places hand to mouth. Reality suddenly fades, and his inner eye envisions the *Zócalo* at the time of the Conquest:

> He sucked blood from his wound and, turning about, let his body drink in the four sides of the great square. It was deserted. The last oblique ray of the sun stood out like a shield. His blood moved with the shifting quickness of mercury . . . . Another image crossed his violently moving eyes: the flow of a dark canal to the south, filled with dark tunics; on the north, a corner where the stone broke into shapes of flaming shafts and red skulls and still butterflies; a wall of snakes between the twin roofs of rain and fire; to the west, the secret castle of albinos and hunchbacks and peacocks' tails and dried eagle heads. The two images, live and dynamic in his eyes, dissolved back and forth into each other, each a bottomless mirror for the reappearance of the other.

Secondly, this type of scene, in which contemporary reality is described with the characteristics of the pre-Hispanic world, fuses the problems of present-day Mexican existence with Aztec metaphor. The Indian view of the cyclical nature of existence, by which earth and sun die each day, only to be resurrected at night's end, is implicit in Ixca's description of his life as "my eternal mortal leap toward tomorrow." The metaphor is perfectly expressive of the anguished impermanence of everyday life in today's hostile environment.

In similar fashion, numerous other Aztec concepts take on modern meaning in the larger context of the novel: the necessity to propitiate the gods via human sacrifice in order to survive; individual destiny as inseparable from the nature of one's origins; subordination of individual personality to the collective. Such themes are interwoven so elusively into the final epilogue that they are suggested rather than delimited, as in the following:

> Lords of the night because we dream in it; Lords of life because we know it to be only a long failure which consists of preparing it and spending it until its end; heart of opening blooms, only you do not need to speak; everything except your voice speaks to us. You have no memory, because life all is lived at the same time; your birthpangs are as long as the sun, as brief as a bunch of grapes; you have learned how to be born every day, to be aware of your nocturnal death; how could you understand one without the other? How could you understand a living hero? The jade knife is long, given to you by the night with its toothless and bleeding mouth; how can you reject the pleas of the night, which are the pleas of your own image? Long is the night and near the hearts, and swift the sacrifice which you execute without compassion, without anger, swift and black, because you ask it of yourself, because you would wish to be that wounded breast, that lifted, flaunted heart—kill it in the spring of resurrections, the eternal spring which does not permit you to count grey hairs, caresses or forebodings; kill him, for he is like unto himself, which means like you, kill him

before he can speak, for the day you hear his voice
you will not be able to resist him, you will feel hatred
and shame and will want to live for him, for you will
not exist and will have no name; kill him and you will
believe in him, kill him and you will have your hero;
pull the coals nearer and nearer to his feet so that his
flesh may rise as high as dust and your own remains
may fly over the valley . . . .

This long epilogue, building through changes of tone
and reference for some fifteen pages, begins with a Joycean
stream of images, followed by a cumulative series of historical and contemporary references. Since narrative subject
and object are both unclear, the effect achieved approaches
that of the collective unconscious of Mexico City, its final
sentence synthesizing an attitude of resignation: "Here we
landed. What can we do about it. Here where the air is
clear." Meanings and implications, oscillating between obscurity and ambiguity in their metaphoric profusion, are in
consonance with Fuentes' imaginative interpretation of
Mexico's past and present.

Ambition certainly exceeded control in the author's effort to explore such a wide gamut of stylistic possibilities.
Obscurity, as in the passage above, is one of the pitfalls. Unevenness and disproportion is a second, as in the long, in-
voluted interior monologues of Rosenda and Mercedes, in
which highly charged subjective language loses its force because the characters themselves are secondary. Verbal excess is evident in many places. Tedium in the overextended
final section is inevitable. But these are lesser considerations,
for indeed the variety of style does make possible the collage structure upon which the novel is built, and the imaginative, poetic qualities of the author's language authenticate

his personalized vision of the complex themes of modern existence, as seen from a Mexican vantage point.

LITERARY INFLUENCES

There are qualities in *Where the Air is Clear* which clearly attest to an awareness of Joyce and Huxley. To these names can be added that of Faulkner, whose indirect presence can be felt in the many long paragraphs of interminable, run-on sentences which heap together ideas and impressions, in a sequence more indicative of emotional patterns beneath the surface than of the logic in the formal concepts expressed. In fact, as indicated earlier, Fuentes personally has acknowledged a sense of identification with the mood of defeat overhanging the novels of Faulkner.[8]

More specific references have been made above to the particular influences of Dos Passos and Arreola. Emir Rodríguez Monegal mentions without elaboration not only Dos Passos, Huxley, and Faulkner, but Alfred Doeblin, Jean-Paul Sartre, and D. H. Lawrence.[9] Many other critics have singled out the obvious presence of Octavio Paz.

But to catalogue influences is to engage in a sterile exercise of questionable value. More important are the questions: to what extent was the author merely copying a particular technique, borrowing an idea or theme? To what extent did he extract the essence of the literary experience, learning from it, absorbing it, and then proceeding to convert it with freshness and originality to his own purposes?

In an interview with Luis Harss and Barbara Dohmann, Fuentes recognized that his novel was technically derivative but felt this to be inevitable and not at all embarrassing to the Latin American novelist, who perhaps out of a sense of cultural inferiority has always felt free to shop abroad for his forms of expression.[10] Fuentes was an exceptionally avid shopper. The question is, to what extent did he shop wisely, and adapt his imports to his own purposes?

A case in point is the Dos Passos influence. Certainly in *Where the Air is Clear* the camera-eye technique effectively broadens novelistic scope, extending outward among human types and varied neighborhoods. It introduces notions of the complexities of existence and succeeds in personalizing larger problems precisely because the vignettes themselves are original and authentic. In addition, they contribute an element of structural coherence which at other times is lacking.

By contrast, the passage expressing Robles' mental flashback by means of garbled headlines, popular song and memory fragments is less effective. The fact that it stands out as a single instance accentuates its experimental quality, ultimately raising the question of why it served in this particular scene and nowhere else. Instead of becoming integrated into the narrative texture, it stands apart, emphasizing the potpourri character of the novel. Here is an example of incorporating an unassimilated technique, copied rather than recreated.

While the mixed blessing of Dos Passos' influence is evident largely in narrative technique, two more substantive sources of inspiration were D. H. Lawrence and Octavio Paz. The former influence provides an example of creative assimilation of subject material by Fuentes. The presence of Paz is especially evident in thematic interpretation and the development of world view.

Ixca Cienfuegos is partially a descendent of *The Plumed Serpent*. A key thread in Lawrence's exotic, romanticised vision of Mexico is the latter-day force of pre-Hispanic myth. The two leading Mexican characters in this novel advocate

and initiate a cult of Quetzalcoatl as the way of salvation for
Mexico of the 1920's—a way to blunt the materialist thrust
of the mass Revolution and renew ties with the spiritual heritage of the Aztecs. In Lawrence's view, this primitive religion lies dormant in the breast of the Mexican Indian who
has never fully accepted Christianity. The novelistic viewpoint is that of an educated Englishwoman whose own dis-
taste for Western hypocrisy, shallow intellectualism, and
crass materialism enables her ultimately to reject her own
cultural background in favor of the compelling and exotic
values she finds in Mexico—religious primitivism, identification with the forces of nature, innocent sexual strength,
and the beauty of mythic symbol and ritual.

A similar theme is present in the personage of Ixca. But
Fuentes' treatment and interpretation depart significantly
from Lawrence's version, which is based on a view of Mexico from the outside. Like the Lawrence characters, Don Ramón and Cipriano, Ixca advocates a reestablishment of ties
with the Indian past. But while the British author projects
this return to an Adamite innocence as a refuge from modern
society and a source of regeneration for Western man, Fuentes' view bears an opposite implication. Ixca represents a
vital current in the contemporary Mexican psyche, a longing
to turn to the past in order to renew bonds which had been
forcibly and traumatically severed. But for Fuentes, this current is not regenerative; its fatalism and hostility must be
accounted for, but its portent is essentially tragic.

While *The Plumed Serpent* constitutes a rather monolithic elaboration of the myth of rebirth, in Fuentes the
theme of sacrifice is counterbalanced by the contemporary
themes of guilt and personal responsibility. The thrust of
Ixca toward the collective past is offset by Zamacona and by
Robles. Lawrence, who was a product of more simplistic pre-

World War II thought, identifies with his protagonist and projects an answer to the moral problem he poses. Fuentes writes from a later, more disillusioned period. Maintaining distance from his characters, he presents the complexity of the dilemma, affirming only the imperative nature of the search. The author partakes of multiple viewpoints and leaves the basic problems unresolved.

The Plumed Serpent was born of a need to synthesize Freud and Frazer (*The Golden Bough*) as an answer to the decadence of modern Europe. Fuentes, formed in an intellectual environment tending away from nationalism, reflects the efforts of intellectuals like Samuel Ramos, Leopoldo Zea, and Octavio Paz to measure Mexican problems on a universal scale. For this reason, Freud and Frazer are also present in *Where the Air is Clear*. But myth and psychology are not sufficient. Fuentes also incorporates a Marxist-influenced view of history as the setting for the character Ixca Cienfuegos. Thus, while Ixca may have been suggested directly or indirectly by Lawrence's novel, Fuentes has situated him in a context based on a different philosophy of history. Further, he has developed Ixca within an author-character relationship of distance rather than identification. The result is a character whose novelistic embodiment and meaning part company with *The Plumed Serpent*.

Another case in point—of similar subject matter but differing interpretations—is the bullfight scene in each novel. In the opening chapter of *The Plumed Serpent*, the Englishwoman Kate reacts with violent emotions against what she finds to be the ugliness and senseless cruelty of a Mexican bullfight. The animosity and the crassness of the huge crowd repel her, as it enjoys the spectacle and the bloodletting with collective relish. Accentuating the unpleasantness is the personal hostility expressed—some in the moblike audience snatch each others' hats and skim them away derisively. Kate's companions are targets for thrown oranges and banana skins, a suggestion of anti-gringo sentiment.

The briefer bullfight scene in *Where the Air is Clear* presents a similarly negative view of the Mexican pastime, barren of any Hemingway-inspired connotations of sport and art. But it is almost as if Fuentes has wished to answer Lawrence, setting forth the underlying reasons for the explosive mass psychology of the moment. For his scene is narrated from the point of view of Gabriel and Beto, through the eyes of characters who epitomize the sordid brutality which so repels Kate in the other novel. In fact, their conduct is even more hostile. They shout insults at bullfighters and gringos, throw objects, frighten people with a live snake, and provoke a fight in which one of them wields a knife.

This scene, however, is one of several in a chapter entitled "Maceualli"—the Aztec term for society's lower class. In the course of the chapter, the reader assembles a larger view of the pattern of existence of Beto and Gabriel, twentieth-century subproletarian *maceualli,* offspring of the generation which fought the Revolution. Their frustrations, their economic hardships as *braceros,* their loss of any notions of citizenship, their vulgar tastes, their dehumanized attitudes towards women, the corruption of their native language—and despite all, their sense of comradeship in suffering—these are complementary to their outrageously antisocial actions at the bullfight. The reader is repelled by their behavior, but he is led to understand it.

In the case of Lawrence, Fuentes has been "influenced" in the sense that he has incorporated similar thematic material, even a similar scene, into *Where the Air is Clear.* However, that theme and scene now bear new values and meanings, performing a different conceptual function within Fuentes' novel.

Turning to Octavio Paz, the echoes of *The Labyrinth of Solitude (El laberinto de la soledad)* resound throughout *Where the Air is Clear,* an influence acknowledged freely by Fuentes himself and widely mentioned by critics. Close inspection reveals that Paz's essays have an unmistakable relationship to many themes.

Published first in 1950 and in expanded form later, *The Labyrinth of Solitude*[11] represents a high point of the post-Revolutionary search among Mexican intellectuals to define in new terms the essence of the national character. This attempt at self-analysis, which began with Samuel Ramos in the mid-1930's, matured two decades later with the series of publications entitled "México y lo mexicano," edited by the philosopher Leopoldo Zea. It also stimulated a series of round-table discussions and debates among writers, academicians, and artists. That Fuentes, who participated in these activities, had them in mind while writing his first novel is very evident in a scene in which Ixca encounters Manuel Zamacona by chance. The latter, who has just emerged from the Palace of Fine Arts, carries books under his arm and one of them is *The Labyrinth of Solitude.* Zamacona explains, in sarcastic terms, the meeting he has just attended:

"A round table discussion on Mexican literature. Should we mention the *serapes* of Saltillo, did Franz Kafka live off a budget from Wall Street, whether social literature is merely the eternal triangle between two Stakhanovites and one tractor, if the more Mexican we are the more universal we become, whether we should write like Buddhists or like Martians. Lots of formulas, no books."

Where the Air is Clear is an attempt to rise above stagnant debate and grapple seriously, through the form of the novel, with the question of *mexicanidad* and the wide range of problems raised by the intellectuals. But more concretely it represents the author's elaboration of many specific themes from these debates and especially from Paz.

The Labyrinth of Solitude is a sweeping analysis of the Mexican psyche, taking into account the phases of national history, applying throughout a dialectical approach, finding parallels between the Freudian problems of the individual and the larger dilemmas which shaped Mexican character.

Within the framework of his interpretations of history, Paz was concerned with identifying the taproots of Mexican culture:

The history of Mexico is the history of a man seeking his parentage, his origins. He has been influenced at one time or another by France, Spain, the United States and the militant indigenists of his own country, and he crosses history like a jade comet, now and then giving off flashes of lightning. What is he pursuing in his eccentric course? He wants to go back beyond the catastrophe he suffered: he wants to be a sun again, to return to the center of that life from which he was separated one day.[12]

More specifically, Paz finds that this same search for roots characterized the Zapatista movement, largely Indian, during the Revolution:

The Zapatista movement attempted to rectify the history of Mexico and the very meaning of our existence as a nation—a program quite different from the historical project of the liberals. The Zapatistas did not conceive of Mexico as a future to be realized but as a return to origins. The radicalism of the Mexican Revolution consisted in its originality, that is, in its return to our roots, the only proper bases for our institutions. When the Zapatistas made the *calpulli* the basic element in our economic and social structure, they not only salvaged the valid portion of the colonial tradition but also affirmed that any political construction, if it is to be truly productive, must derive from the most ancient, stable and lasting part of our national being: the indigenous part.[13]

This is the same theme which Ixca Cienfuegos represents, both in his thinking about national destiny and his relations with other characters. A dialogue with Zamacona illustrates the theme in national terms: (the following omits descriptive passages to focus on the spoken interchange)

"And this is a country that has already been violated too many times. It that what you want to tell me?"

"No," said Ixca, "Only once."

"When?"

"When it forgot that the first decision is the last, that you can't go beyond that original disposition, because all the others are just disguises."

"What original decision?"

"The decision of the first Mexico, the Mexico tied to its own umbilical cord, the Mexico that really was an incarnation of ritual, that built itself upon faith, that . . ."

". . . that really was under the heel of a bloody despotism, concealed by a satanic theology . . ."

"And power today? In a few minutes Federico Robles is going to join us. Today he commands, or did command, power. Do you think his cheap marketplace power, without any greatness, is better than a power which at least had the imagination to ally itself with the great forces, permanent and inviolable, of the cosmos? With the sun itself? I tell you I'd rather die immolated on a sacrificial stone than buried under the excrement of capitalist tricks and newspaper gossip."

On a personal level, Ixca applies the same principle of evaluating individuals in terms of their continuity with their decisive origins. Thus, Robles' personality evades Ixca because the all-important key to its origin is unclear:

Robles was the enigma, the unfathomable, master of the new Mexican world before which Norma and Rodrigo kneeled; more than others he was its slave and its rebel . . . the only one who had known or sensed domains vaster in origin and contrasting against the world which today constricted them all. And what was the origin, the real origin of Robles? Ixca . . . knew that in some way it had to be so simple that he, Ixca, would never understand it. The dark, marginal life that Hortensia Chacón offered him was a substitute, at most a faint reflection of that original encounter. The use of power described by Librado Ibarra, and also by Robles himself was only a flight from, and at the same time a restructuring of, that same hidden origin. And in the destiny that that origin was to encounter, Ixca now felt, there the battle would be fought . . . .

To Paz, the past is still a living phenomenon, immutable and permanent, though perhaps it has been covered over with modern institutions. He states:

> Past epochs never vanish completely, and blood still drips from all their wounds, even the most ancient. Sometimes the most remote or hostile beliefs and feelings are found together in one city or one soul . . . .[14]
>
>   . . . . .
>
> Any contact with the Mexican people, however brief, reveals that the ancient beliefs and customs are still in existence beneath Western forms. These still-living remains testify to the vitality of the pre-Cortesian cultures.[15]

Much of the brilliant imagery of Fuentes, translating modern environment and contemporary relationships in passages laden with Aztec metaphors, elaborates this theme from Paz in literary terms. At one moment, Ixca verbalizes it with unmistakable clarity:

> "There's nothing indispensable in Mexico, Rodrigo. Sooner or later, a secret, anonymous force inundates it and transforms it all. It's a force that's older than all memory, as reduced and concentrated as a grain of powder: it's the origin. All the rest is a masquerade. The origin, that's where Mexico still is, and that's what it is, never what it can become. Mexico is something fixed forever, incapable of evolution. A mother rock that resists everything."

Another theme emerges from this persistent analysis of the multiple meanings of the past: the linking of today's sense of defeat, both national and personal, with the traumatic defeats of Mexican history, particularly the over-whelming defeat of the Aztecs. Paz discusses this tendency in terms of the Freudian death-wish which triumphs over the dialectically opposed drive for survival:

> The duality of Aztec religion, reflected in its theocratic-military division and its social system, corresponds to the contradictory impulses that motivate all human be-ings and groups. The death-wish and the will-to-live conflict in each one of us. These profound tendencies impregnate the activities of all classes, castes, and indi-viduals, and in critical moments they reveal themselves in complete nakedness. The victory of the death-wish shows that the Aztec suddenly lost sight of their destiny. Cuauhtémoc fought in the knowledge that he would be defeated. The nature of this struggle lies in this bold and intimate acceptance of defeat.[16]

In *Where the Air is Clear,* the experience of defeat is decisive for all of the leading characters. Ixca's attempt to regain the past is ultimately fruitless. The idealism of Zama-cona meets senseless death. Rodrigo admits finally that he has forsaken his cherished personal goals. For Robles, defeat proves to be purgative and restorative, and of all the desti-nies, his appears to come to terms with defeat, as it impels him to rearrange his outlook and reorder his existence. The defeat which closes the doors of the capitalist world to him seems to be followed at the novel's end by a search for a new life.

Early in the novel, Zamacona meditates on the defeats in Mexican history and their possible value, in a passage close to the concepts of Paz, a passage which foreshadows the later career of Robles:

"Would Mexico accept itself in victory? We savor
and we take seriously only our defeats. Victories we tend
to convert into empty holidays, like the 5th of May. But
the Conquest, the war with the United States . . .
Who really won the war of 1847? The apparent victory
of the United States, Mexicans think without saying it,
was the triumph of brute force, drunken power, materialism and excessive growth. Human values lost out
. . . . Mass-produced automobiles versus folk handi-
crafts. Etc., etc. Mexico's defeat, on the other hand,
leads us to truth, to values, to knowledge of the limitations appropriate to men of culture and good will. What
succeeds is not always what is valuable, but rather the
contrary."

Against the tendency to turn from the present to the
past, to measure the present only as a reflection of the past,
are posed the various ways in which post-Revolutionary
Mexico sees itself as emerging from the dark forest of former
suffering into the modern daylight of the world community.
This does not imply severing the connections with antiquity,
but returning to it in order to understand it, to assimilate it,
and thus to transcend it. Paz sees the Revolution as a phase
in the dialectical pattern of Mexican history:

If we contemplate the Mexican Revolution in terms of
the ideas outlined in this essay, we see that it was a
movement attempting to reconquer our past, to assimilate it and make it live in the present. This will to return, the consequence of solitude and desperation, is
one of the phases of that dialectic of solitude and communion, reunion and separation, which seems to rule
our whole history. Thanks to the Revolution, the Mexican wants to reconcile himself with his history and his

origins. This explains why the character of the movement is both desperate and redemptive.[17]

Essentially the same idea is voiced by Manuel Zamacona during a heated interchange with Robles. The latter, at
the height of his power as an industrialist, argues that the
past is dead and must be buried. The new Mexico must now
raise itself to economic prosperity or perish. "Our only
choice is between wealth or misery. And to attain wealth we
have to hasten our steps towards capitalism, and adjust everything to that system. Politics. Style of living. Tastes. Leg-
islation. Economy. Everything you can mention." Mockingly
he asks if Zamacona would prefer to return to Indian primitivism, and the latter, in an echo of Paz, sets out the need
for cultural and historic continuity as the basis for maintaining national identity while at the same time confronting the
modern world:

> "What I want is that the shadows of the past no longer
> rob us of sleep. I want to understand what it meant to
> wear feathers in order not to wear them, in order to be
> myself. I don't want us to delight in mourning the past,
> but to penetrate it, understand it, reduce it to reason,
> cancel out what is dead, save that part which is living,
> and know at last what Mexico really is and what can be
> done with her."

A moment later in the same discussion, he describes
how the Revolution illuminates the past:

> "Without the Revolution neither you nor I would be
> here talking this way; I mean, without the Revolution,
> we never would have faced the problem of Mexico's
> meaning, its past. It's as though in the Revolution all
> the great men of our history reappear, carrying their

burdens. I really feel that in the faces of the Revolution all of them come back, with their grossness and their refinement, their rhythms, their voices and colors. But if the Revolution reveals all our history for us, it doesn't guarantee that we'll understand it or be able to rise above it."

Specific qualities of Mexican personality are identified in the Paz analysis of contemporary Mexican character. His examination of "machismo"—the aggressive, "closed," masculine attitude which has a counterpart in the "openness" of the female figure who lies dormant, waiting to be awakened and made vibrant by the male—is embodied in the relationship between Robles and Hortensia.

Further, there are masks behind which Mexicans hide their intimate feelings, according to Paz. One is that of the dissembler, who constantly varies his outward role in society, adjusting his defense mechanism to exterior pressures. Such a character is Rodrigo Pola. Never in control of his own personality, he alternates between playing the ridiculous fool and attempting to achieve the upper hand over Norma and those of her social circle, all the while hiding his personal bitterness. At one point in the novel, he writes, in the form of a personal diary, an essay on his own oscillating identity, seeking to define the relationship between the mask and the true personality. A passage from the six-page, first-person treatise establishes its Paz-like conception:

"It can happen that the game, the artifice, by dint of so much repetition, comes to be what is authentic, and that the original personality is lost forever, atrophied from lack of use. I don't know. One thing certain is that, carried along by this personal dialectic, I no longer know which is my true mask."

The chapter from *The Labyrinth of Solitude* on "The Day of the Dead" and the significance of the fiesta in the Mexican pattern of existence finds literary interpretation in Fuentes' chapter on the fiesta of September 15. Paz sees the institution of the fiesta as a rupture of solitude, the moment when the Mexican breaks out of the enclosure of personal isolation into communion with society, frequently in tumult and violence. "This is the night when friends who have not exchanged more than the prescribed courtesies for months get drunk together, trade confidences, weep over the same troubles, discover that they are brothers, and sometimes, to prove it, kill each other."[18]

Just such an atmosphere prevails in the Fuentes chapter, which in the context of the novel sets up an appropriate frame of explosiveness for the violent deaths of Gabriel and Manuel Zamacona. At one moment, a drunken dialogue between Gabriel and Beto brings to life Paz's description:

> "Sure, Gabriel. On the night of the fifteenth, everything comes back to you. You need to tell things to your buddies and get 'em off your chest." Beto tilted his glass and shook his head. "Every kick in the teeth you ever had . . . . Every memory that makes you want to cry."
>
> "You said it. Suffer, man. If you can't talk to your buddies, who else is there? I swear to God, Beto, you're my true brother and I love you."

With regard to broader philosophical reflections, such as the nature of history and myth, there is also a relationship in the thinking of Paz and Fuentes, although less specific. Fuentes' interpretation of these subjects must be extrapolated from literary values, rather than from particular narrative passages.

Concerning the value of history as a tool for understanding man, Paz has decided reservations. He repeatedly states its limitations:

> Man is not simply the result of history and the forces that activate it, as is now claimed; nor is history simply the result of the human will, a belief on which the North American way of life is implicitly predicated. Man, it seems to me, is not *in* history: he *is* history.[19]
>
> .   .   .   .   .
>
> This is to say that historical events are something more than events because they are coloured by humanity, which is always problematical. And they are not merely the result of other events, but rather of a single will that is capable, within certain limits, of ruling their outcome. History is not a mechanism, and the influences among diverse components of an historical event are reciprocal . . . Historical circumstances explain our character to the extent that our character explains those circumstances. Both are the same. Thus any purely historical explanation is insufficient . . . which is not the same as saying that it is false.[20]

Reservations notwithstanding, Paz proceeds to treat Mexican history in the light of the dialectic of solitude and communion. The Conquest was a rupture for the Indian, analogous to the break between child and mother, leaving the Aztecs orphaned by their gods. The colonial period achieved a degree of stability because of the universality of the church, which offered a shelter, and also because of the positive heritage from the Spanish Renaissance. The stagnation and decadence of the baroque period led to a new outburst, the popular movement for independence. And when independence proved to be stagnant itself, the decisive explosion of the Reform ensued. This was a triple rupture: with the Spanish heritage, with the Indian past, with Catholicism —the traditions which had inclined the Mexican toward communion. But the resultant straitjacket, the distortion of liberalism into *porfirismo* again left the Mexican alone, cut off from the resources of the past. The Revolution came partly from the need to reestablish ties with historical traditions and forms. Paz sees this need as only partly fulfilled, leaving Mexico in an undecided state, torn between past and future, between nationalism and universality, between agrarianism and industrialization, and between solitude and communion.

In addition, he views man as torn by the dichotomy between chronometric time and mythological time, a dichotomy "expressed in the opposition between history and myth."[21]

> Mythical time—father of all times that mask reality— coincides with our inner, subjective time. Man, the prisoner of succession, breaks out of his invisible jail and enters living time: his subjective life becomes identical with exterior time . . . . Myths and fiestas, whether secular or religious, permit man to emerge from his solitude and become one with creation. Therefore myth—disguised, obscure, hidden—reappears in almost all our acts and intervenes decisively in our history . . . .[22]

All of these questions—the tensions between myth and history, between subjective and objective time, between past and present, personal identity and collective character, internal life and social relationships—enter into the world view which Carlos Fuentes projects in *Where the Air is Clear*.

WORLD VIEW

National consciousness is by far the most important focus through which the novel structures a view of man's existence. "Who are we Mexicans?" Fuentes is asking. If he can answer that question, perhaps he can also answer the other that faces all modern man, "Who am I?" He approaches the question from various points of view, as befits a post-World War II writer, and also as befits a spokesman for the agonized debates of the new intellectuals.

The most determined and persistent speaker, Ixca, represents the collectivist viewpoint. "Tie ourselves to the cosmos" is his watchword. He is a representative of bedrock *indigenismo,* obdurate in his insistence on the power of primitivism, viewing the Mexicans as incapable of reconciliation with change from the Conquest through the Revolution.

His opposite is Robles, a modern tycoon who evokes both his own revolutionary sacrifice and the future of Mexico as justifications for wealth, power, and personal gratifications. But he is more than a capitalist caricature because of the "other side," with which he finally comes to grips after his downfall. His future is vague and ambivalent, like Mexico's.

The intellectual Zamacona advocates penetration of the past as a guide to solving contemporary problems, and undoing traditional wrongs. He would take into account cultural uniqueness in order to arrive at creative solutions for post-Revolutionary problems. He attempts to bridge the static conservatism of Ixca's current with the dynamism of Robles. He is the intellectual speaking, posing questions, trying to understand, seeing many sides to an issue, himself immobilized and indecisive.

Lesser spokesmen add to the complexity of the question, "Who are we Mexicans?" There is the romanticist, Rodrigo, whose idealized self-image capitulates to material enticements. Norma is a courtesan with flair, a parasitic product who reveals, when challenged by Ixca, the core of corruption beneath the decorative facade. She is another image of modern Mexico. The *mujeres sufridas,* Rosenda and Hortensia, are both trying to make a life out of suffering the injustices that men have inflicted. One approaches her task negatively, the other positively. The *maceualli* are the masses, the eternally *chingados.* They are bitter and unable to overcome the frustrations that poverty and oppression impose, but they are vital and human.

With minor characters and vignettes added to create a city-scape, which, in turn, is a reflection of that which is most vital in Mexico today, Fuentes is not only asking— "Who are we?"—but answering with, "Whoever we are, we've got to learn to live with it."

Here's where we landed. What can we do about it. Here where the air is clear.

There is no question mark in these last lines. It is a statement of fact. The novel's message, if any, is a cry to come to grips with nationhood, in order to cope with present day reality. It is a recognition of diversity, of varied interests of individual Mexicans, of complexity. It runs counter to official pronouncements—"un sólo camino"[23]—which may, like Robles, justify maintaining those in the saddle. The Mexico of *Where the Air is Clear* is not a simple nation, and for her problems there are no simple answers.

Further, Fuentes sees the sophisticated world of post-Revolutionary Mexico in many ways as a prisoner of myth.

He poses the static against the changing, the mystical against the rational. The "origins" which Ixca seeks are counterposed to fast-moving Western culture; the echoes of the Indian presence remain in conflict with imported values. It is a view of life that contains a Jungian collective consciousness, affecting both individuals and the nation.

A theme which speaks to this darker side is the repeated motif of sacrifice. From Teódula's drive to propitiate the Aztec gods, Ixca's obsession to carry out her wishes, to Zamacona's formulation—"There has been no successful hero in Mexico. To be heroes, they have had to perish: Cuauhtémoc, Hidalgo, Madero, Zapata. Cortés, the hero who triumphs, is not accepted as such"—the idea of sacrifice is a concept repeated with mythic overtones.

A related mythic component is the view of life as a constant process of rebirth, and history as reduced to a record of cyclical transition from stage to stage of the same endless pattern. Ixca refers in the very first paragraph to "my eternal mortal leap toward tomorrow," embodying the sense of changelessness which characterizes a sentence in the final poetic ode to Mexico City: "You have no memory, for everything lives at the same time."

Mythical underpinning, reinforced by a torrential flow of poetic imagery, provides an echo of Rulfo's projection of Mexican existence as congealed in an archetypally fixed structure. Implicit is the tragic suggestion that the national makeup, bowed down by an undying sense of defeat which originated in the trauma of the Conquest, is basically unchangeable.

But unlike Rulfo, Fuentes does not stop there. Myth is one side of the coin; the other displays modern Western rationalism with a strong component of Karl Marx. The Revolution itself comes under close scrutiny. By contrast with

Yáñez, who returns to the *porfiriato* to examine the stages of revolutionary imminence, Fuentes is mostly concerned with assaying the ultimate results, from the vantage point of the post-Revolution.

On balance, his view, while not final, tends to be sharply critical as he details a movement which, he implies, has institutionalized itself, undergoing political and social hardening of the arteries. Zamacona, speaking for his generation, criticizes the status of the nation which it inherited from those who actually fought the battles:

> "It's not the same for us, sir. You had urgent tasks before you, and your own rise was rapid, as you kept pace with their fulfillment. We've found ourselves in another country, stable and rigid, where everything is pretty much settled and taken care of, where it's very hard to have any influence in public matters. A country jealous of its *status quo*. Sometimes I think Mexico is living a prolonged *Directory*, a formula for stability that, while it keeps internal peace, prevents the meaningful development of exactly what the Revolution proposed in the beginning."

The view of the power structure which the novel presents is indeed a desolate one, notwithstanding the air of dynamism and activity which pervades the background of Mexico City. The *nouveau riche* class of Robles, and of the financiers who cause his ruin, is imbued with a combined sense of righteousness and power as its members identify the nation's interests with their own. The working poor, on the other end of the widening social spectrum, remain disinherited, eking out subsistence in an atmosphere of personal tension, suffering, and violence. The intellectuals, heirs to the revolutionary tradition, have little autonomy, as Zamacona indicates, in words which express the author's discontent:

> And the intellectuals, who could be a moral counterpoint to this force which overpowers us—well, there they are, more dead from fear than a kidnapped virgin. The Revolution was identified with the intellectual force which Mexico generated from within itself . . . just as it was close to the workers' movement. But when the Revolution stopped being a revolution, both intellectuals and workers found that they were now official movements."

In counterpoint to the vision of a nation's reliving in contemporary garb the forms and patterns of the pre-Hispanic past, the novel projects a modern interpretation of history. Octavio Paz has stated, ". . . I am not suggesting that we abandon the old methods or reject Marxism, at least as an instrument for historical analysis."[24] With this Carlos Fuentes would seem to agree, particularly in his analysis of the Revolution as an historical phenomenon. The early Federico Robles, for example, who states a rationale for the emergence of a neo-capitalist state out of the ashes of bloody rebellion, is a projection of the author's critical estimate that the Revolution brought about a realignment of the nation's political and economic structure, not necessarily positive in value. Further evidence of his unfavorable judgment of this newly formed neo-capitalism is found in the mordant portrait of parasitic pseudo-intelligentsia inhabiting the cocktail-party world of the metropolis.

History in *The Edge of the Storm* is interpreted as a dialectical process containing patterns of both repetition and change. This tendency is present in *Where the Air is Clear*, but Fuentes complicates his vision, suggesting historical tensions on many planes. By the novel's end, it is clear that neither the Revolution nor personal sacrifices have accomplished much. One group of oppressors has replaced another. Zamacona has died in vain and Ixca himself rejects his mother's solution. This leaves the problem, "whither Mexico?" up in the air, which is anything but transparent, ideologically or otherwise. Only Robles may have discovered something, but Fuentes must not be too sure of what it is, for it is never revealed to the reader.

All this emphasis on the national dilemma reflects, as stated earlier, the discussions on *autognosis* personified by Octavio Paz and Leopoldo Zea. Fuentes creates individuals out of Paz's Mexican types, weaves a story out of his own generation's national preoccupations, builds dreams out of the tensions between Paz's dialectical opposites, solitude and communion.

What light does this focus shed upon the Mexican *condition humaine*? It reveals contemporary man torn between past and present, struggling to establish a sense of historical continuity, oscillating between the solitude of Pola and the collectivism of Cienfuegos, between the rocklike sameness of inherited mythic formulations of the cosmos and the kaleidoscopic changes by which world history now impinges on national destiny.

The Mexican response to these dichotomies, epitomized by Rodrigo's repertory of masks, is to alternate in a Paz-like pattern of behavior on both personal and mass levels—between hermetic withdrawal and infrequent but explosive communion. Modern alienation and dog-eat-dog competition for survival are contrasted with the sacrifice theme, and the solidarity of the *maceualli*.

The search for origins imparts an ethnocentric cast to this quest for national identity. Ixca, naturally, is the vehicle for most variations on the theme. In his interpretation Mexico is the navel of man's existence, and he extends the concept to see his nation as the center of all man's hopes, because it epitomizes suffering and because it has never cast off its remote past:

> "Salvation for the whole world depends upon this anonymous people who are at the center, the very navel of the planet. Mexico's people, the only ones who are contemporaneous with the world itself, the only ones who live with their teeth fastened to the original breast. This mass of stink and cankers and scummy pulque and rotting bodies that wallow in the undifferentiated muck of their origin. Today all the others are falling toward that origin which, without their knowing it, controls them; only we have always lived in it."
>
> .　.　.　.　.
>
> "And in that origin, Zamacona, they will know that there has been no suffering, no defeat, no pain comparable to those of Mexico. And there they will know that if Mexicans are not to be saved, not one single being in all creation will be saved."

This culture-centered view, which sees Mexican self-identification as the burning issue of the day, dates the book even within the national literature. Nevertheless, it is a valiant attempt to put into novelistic form the obsession of that period with national psychoanalysis.

Despite the self-conscious national focus, however, the novel establishes a clear link with Western post-World War II existential thought. The sense of responsibility of individual and nation, rooted in the anguished consciousness of past failures, merges with that of Western man. The world view of *Where the Air is Clear* is modern precisely because it of-

fers no clear-cut answers, because it is willing to come to
grips with dilemmas without solution, because it is nondidac-
tic and ambiguous, and because it presents its material from
multiple viewpoints. And, in keeping with the modern novel
from Joyce to Camus, the more self-knowledge man achieves,
the more painful his doubts become.

Commanding no final answers, Fuentes cannot assume
the Olympian stance of the storyteller who is in possession
of all the facts. His narrative perspective situates him in
Mexico City, a shift of locus from rural to urban, for the contemporary metropolis lends itself to the treatment of modern, universal questions. He is a contemporary of Robles,
Ixca, and Rodrigo. Like them he is working out his destiny,
and like their lives, his novel bears a final interpretation
which is ambiguous. The painful doubts persist.

Man in his environment is the universal theme, or the
"man-not-in-history, man-is-history" formulation of Octavio
Paz. Fuentes tries to make us view each character within the
total picture, with each part interrelated and interdependent,
from the street sweeper to the banker on top. All are conceived as part of the collage—each action of one affecting
the others. Although this plan is not fully accomplished, he
attempts to make it all of a piece.

One source of contemporary anguish is the relative absence of freedom of choice for the individual in such a complex of pressures, each disputing for influence. Caught between a crossfire of impulses which operate on his makeup
—the mythical currents of his culture, the relentless cycles
of national history, origins which determine later destiny,
the heavy inheritance of guilt to be assumed—the individual
finds limited scope for personal development, for maturation
of individual personality.

The weblike interaction makes the environment almost

a prison. This view impels Fuentes to center his narrative on the collective drama which lies behind the destiny of individual characters, and to adjust their individual psychologies in the interests of the larger questions he seeks to confront. Zamacona's individualism is doomed, Robles tumbles from his position as top dog, and Ixca's dream of a simpler society dissolves into nothingness.

Yet the results are not purely negative. The vitality, the ability to take it (*aguantar*), is a strength of Mexico and of Fuentes' characters. They make out of hardship a blessing, out of defeat, moral victory. In Zamacona's words: "Mexico's defeat . . . leads us to truth, to values, to knowledge of the limitations appropriate to men of culture and good will." There is a redeeming talent in most of the characters of *Where the Air is Clear*. They penetrate their own weaknesses and defeats to make a purging of them. This gives them strength and endurance—the ability to survive, the essential element of humanity. One ends up respecting most of them. One ends by believing Mexico will survive—despite itself.

5 | THE FIELD OF CHOICE: CARLOS FUENTES

The Death of Artemio Cruz
(La muerte de Artemio Cruz)

FOR CARLOS FUENTES, *Where the Air is Clear* served as a proving ground, a laboratory of the novel in which the author could test his talent in assembling literary influences and experimental techniques, in interpreting social realities and intellectual polemics. His next large-scale effort, *The Death of Artemio Cruz,[1]* builds upon this acquired experience but differs significantly from the first novel in technique and in world view. Certainly it retains a preoccupation with the Revolution, as narrative scenes ultimately merge in a sequence ranging from the first decade of the century through the sixth, and as flashback references bring into play historical antecedents of the Santa Anna period, the Juárez Reform movements, and the Díaz dictatorship.

Further, Federico Robles is clearly the literary antecedent of Artemio Cruz, Mexican revolutionary turned bourgeois captain of the post-Revolution. As in the case of Robles, the career of Artemio Cruz springs from the most humble provincial beginnings, followed by initial education from
a mentor (in this case, an anticlerical teacher), then the
headlong plunge into the capricious fortunes of revolutionary combat. Similarly, when the battles are over, the protagonist embarks upon a steady ascent to the top of the post-
Revolutionary financial and social pyramid—an ascent
marked by sordid manipulation and the betrayal of the initial aims and ideals for which the Revolution stood.

But in tone and in form, the present novel treads distinctly new ground. Its entire setting is pervaded by the aura
of death. In this peculiarly penetrating light, the personality
of the dying Artemio Cruz is refracted as he contemplates
and questions the meaning of his life. Thus one life story
constitutes the central thread which was absent in the earlier work. In a sequence of narration determined by the painful mental leaps of an agonized mind, back and forth in time,
a series of random, seemingly chaotic glimpses of the past
gradually fall into order and interrelationship. The complex,
contradictory personality of Artemio Cruz emerges in a portrait which Carlos Fuentes paints with both deep contempt
and sensitive understanding, even compassion.

Unlike *Where the Air is Clear,* in which a loosely constructed narrative montage achieved a large-scale panoramic
view of Mexican society, emphasizing its cultural and historical underpinnings, *The Death of Artemio Cruz* stresses
one individual psychology, one destiny, traced out against
the kaleidoscopic changes of twentieth-century Mexico.
Each fragment of the protagonist's life which is called forth
represents a crucial moment of choice. Frequently the deci-

sions must resolve crises in his personal rather than his public life: there is a decision to avoid a firing squad by revealing information about troop movements; another decision to marry Catalina, sister of Gonzalo Bernal, who had died a martyr before the same firing squad. With Gonzalo dead, Artemio Cruz ruthlessly assumes control of the Bernal family fortunes as a springboard to power, but in the process sacrifices the possibility of winning love from a subjugated wife left to the combined tortures of guilt, resentment, and desire. A further decision is to take his son from an overly protective mother and expose him to the freedom which he, Artemio Cruz, had known as a youth on a Veracruz plantation—resulting in the son's filling out the destiny his father had forsaken. Lorenzo Cruz dies a hero's death with the Spanish Loyalists while his father continues along the corrupt path to personal power.

The imminence of death removes doubts from the reader's mind about how the novel will end. Suspense and dramatic tension stem instead from shifting temporal references and from an ingenious system of changing points of view.

Action is related in rotating order, in fragments of first-person, stream-of-consciousness monologue of the dying man; in a second-person future—with a mysterious other voice, akin to his alter ego, which addresses him, surprisingly, in the future tense while referring to events of the past; and in a traditional third-person preterite, with an omniscient narration recounting crucial flashback scenes which bring to life critical moments of the protagonist's career. The reader then must adjust to the cycles of first-, second-, and third-person narrations, and the continual change of viewpoint which results.

The first-person perspective, with Artemio Cruz in

effect speaking directly to the reader, focuses on his immediate deathbed consciousness. Acute awareness of unpleasant physical sensations and painful body functions reinforces his negative thoughts about family, priest, and associates who visit the sickroom. The greed, hypocrisy, and guilt which he finds in them are counterparts to his own discomfort and, on a deeper level, his own guilt.

In the second-person passages, the reader is a witness as the alter ego voice addresses Cruz, speaking of what has already transpired in the future tense, as though foretelling it. The effect is to place the reader alongside Cruz as he relives his personal crises—as though they had not yet occurred and choices were still open. From this vantage point the reader can participate with the protagonist and thus identify with his dilemma.

The more traditional third-person sequences are the longest. Here the author, through an omniscient narrator, recounts directly to the reader fragments of the protagonist's past, pinpointed exactly in time: July 6, 1941, May 20, 1919, and so on. This constitutes, as it were, "outside" information which can be accepted as an authentic version of the circumstances surrounding the various personal decisions. In several of these sections, the narrative artistry of Fuentes stands out sharply, so that the passages appear almost as finished short stories.

The tension created by varying perspectives is heightened by the nonchronological nature of the narrative sequence, as third-person sections evoke the protagonist's career in hopscotch order. While the reader is aware from the first pages that Artemio Cruz is about to die, only the final section recounting his childhood days fully illuminates the life gradually shaped in the preceding sections, and the death which inevitably ensues.

The net effect of this careful—and artful—handling of structure and point of view is to create a tight, closed, narrative whole, which focuses inward upon its own self-contained complexities rather than projecting outward and depending upon social and historical realities outside the novel.

The history of Mexico is an important presence, however, providing the backdrop for Artemio Cruz's career and imposing the field of choice which he confronts at each juncture. But it is presented with finality, already structured, rather than being analyzed in terms of causality, or developing in the process of the novel. Once again, the process of history is seen as cyclical, involving a pattern of convulsive change which in the end proved to be tragically repetitious. The process is summed up in the thoughts of the elder Bernal, whose family had enriched itself by profiting from the Juárez reforms, accumulating former church-held properties which in turn pass to the grasp of Artemio Cruz under the false banner of revolutionary land reform:

> "Ill-fated country," the old man said to himself as he walked toward his library . . . ; "ill-fated country that with each generation must destroy its old possessors and substitute new masters, just as rapacious and ambitious as those who went before."

Against this backdrop stands the fully rounded figure of Artemio Cruz, a character both admirable in his forcefulness and pathetic in his anguish. On him—his psychology and the meaning of life—falls the major emphasis of the novel, and through him Fuentes elaborates a range of meaningful themes.

If one can say that in good measure *Where the Air is Clear* attempts to answer the generic question, "What does it

mean to be a Mexican?", the underlying problem to which
The Death of Artemio Cruz is addressed can be phrased in
more specific terms: "What chance does the individual find
for personal fulfillment in modern Mexico?"

The construction of the latter novel lends itself to an
existentially oriented view of man. One component of this
view is the concept of life as a series of choices by which
man determines his destiny, a theme repeated throughout
the novel and one which controls the very structure chosen
by the author. An example of the protagonist's thoughts as
he relives the past:

> "You will never need, nor will you have left over, one
> additional chance to make of your life what you want
> it to be. And if you are to be one thing and not another,
> it will be because, despite everything, you will have to
> choose. Your choices will not deny the rest of your
> possible life, all that you will leave behind each time
> you choose—they will only narrow it down, they'll
> shave it thinner to the point where today your choice
> and your destiny will be one and the same. The coin
> will no longer show heads or tails. Your wish will be
> the same as your destiny."

The measure of man is the shape of his life, the value
he infuses into it. And the point at which final judgment
becomes applicable is death. Unlike *Pedro Páramo*, in
which life is merely a prefiguring of death, *The Death of
Artemio Cruz* construes life as the embodiment of all meaning and death as its total negation.

Artemio Cruz suffers existential anguish, tinged with a
number of particular shadings. He is conscious that his destiny is final, but at the same time incomplete. There is a

sense of guilt at having used other individuals, especially his son, as building blocks for his own career ("You will leave behind the useless deaths, the dead names, the names of all those who had to die so that yours could live, the names of those who were dispossessed in order for you to possess . . . ."). Indirectly present is the realization, expressed through desperate blasphemy, of the need for a Supreme Being. Religion had been a phenomenon he never could rely upon for sustenance because the affirmation of life required the negation of godliness ("To live is to betray your God; each act of your life, each act which affirms us as living beings, makes us violate the commandments of your God"). He had the bitter consciousness that life is unfair, that choices are always between more or less evil alternatives:

> "You will think about the fact that one cannot choose, one should not choose, that on that day you didn't choose—you let things happen, you weren't responsible, for you didn't create either of the two moralities which that day were being asked of you. You couldn't be responsible for options you had no part in defining . . . you'll dream of an orderly life, created by you yourself, that you'll never be able to tell about, because the world will never give you a chance, because the world will only offer you its established rules, its own conflicting codes . . ."

All these bits of self-knowledge, as well as recognition of the fallibility in the world around him, contribute to the anguish which makes him a tragic character in the modern sense.

WORLD VIEW

The novel again projects a view of man not as maker of history, but as *in history*, following the conception of Octavio Paz. History is not just a tapestry against which personal drama is enacted, it also is the field of force, restricting individual movement and freedom of choice. Man is tied to circumstance, but the ties are unfortunate.

The cyclical finality with which Carlos Fuentes interprets Mexican history is only partly Marxist oriented. The recurring emergence of new groups to control Mexican society can be explained, he implies, in terms which are primarily based in economics, relating to control of the land and exploitation of the peasant and working classes. Nowhere is this more evident than in the rise of Artemio Cruz to power, first by distorting land reform, then by accumulating real estate and allying himself with foreign (American) investors in lucrative arrangements which depend on strike-breaking, selfish exploitation of the nation's mineral resources, and manipulation of public opinion through a controlled press. The implication is inescapable that the Revolution is no longer an arena of contention, as in *Where the Air is Clear*, between newly arisen dynamic forces, but that the new industrialist class which Cruz represents has completely captured the post-Revolution, crystallizing national patterns definitively into a neo-capitalist mold. This economic determinism is less positive, more fatalistic. Fuentes does not view the capitalist class differently from a Marxist, but there is no emerging working class conscious of or ready to throw off its chains.

In this context, the quest for national self-knowledge, for defining in cultural terms the limits of *mexicanidad*, becomes a secondary problem, subordinate to the more universal burdens imposed by contemporary society on an individualized man who now is more self-aware, more alone, more conscious of the contradictions and imperfections of his own unique psychological makeup. For this reason Fuentes undoubtedly chose to fashion the family background of Artemio Cruz from *criollo* and mulatto antecedents, diluting the immediate relationship in the protagonist with Indian culture, and placing [...] on his contemporary condition[...]

The one maj[...] [...]-
Indian cultural pa[...]
centers on the theme [...]
devotes several brilliant pa[...] [...]e.
Transposing into contemporary [...] [...]al conception that all Mexicans are sons of [...] [...]da—fruit of the violation of a suffering mother by a brutal, anonymous father—Fuentes finds the world of human relationships in which Artemio Cruz moves to be dominated by the code, "Violate your fellow man or be violated yourself." Thus, a political associate tells Cruz:

> "And don't you and I belong among the real sons of bitches? [*chingones*] Understand? Always pick your friends from the sons of bitches, because if you're with them, nobody can screw you. Let's drink."
> They drank, and the fat man explained that this world is divided into sons of bitches and poor bastards, and one has to choose sides.

In a particular passage directly inspired in Paz, Fuentes explores the colloquial and vulgar variations in common speech on the theme of *la chingada,* as Artemio Cruz bitterly takes stock of its negative presence in his own life and the lives around him: "*la chingada,* who poisons love, melts friendship, crushes tenderness, *la chingada* who divides, *la chingada* who separates, *la chingada* who destroys, *la chingada* who corrupts . . . ." The context endows this inherited cultural pattern with contemporary meaning, as the *chingones* ("sons of bitches") become the new ruling class and the "poor bastards" the exploited masses.

Ultimately the estimate of man's situation which Fuentes compiles is measured in relativistic terms. An imperfect being, he is thrown into an imperfect world and forced to make definitive choices in situations of climactic pressure which he will be able to understand and evaluate only much later. Capable of deep love, indeed thirsting for love as was Artemio Cruz, he also houses an inner drive toward evil acts which, in the end, destroy both others and self. Fuentes presents us with a man who evokes both scorn and sympathy, confounding easy moral judgment, and addressing the reader with essentially the same desperate plea which Artemio vainly directed to his alienated wife:

> "I can tell you of those who died because I washed my hands of them, just shrugged my shoulders. Accept me as I am, with this guilt, look upon me as a man in need . . . . Don't hate me. Have mercy, my beloved. Because I love you. Measure on the one hand my guilt and on the other my love, and you'll see that the love is greater . . . ."

By comparison with the uneven first novel, *The Death of Artemio Cruz is* the work of a more accomplished literary craftsman. It is a tightly knit, finished product, depending more fully on form and technique to reveal and interpret its world. Gone are the essay passages and the debates in which characters argue abstract questions. In their place is the treatment of many of the same questions, as posed by the life of a more fully developed protagonist.

This is not to say that the novel is a uniformly tooled masterpiece. There are individual scenes which, in their conception, border dangerously on romantic melodrama: the early love of the protagonist for Regina, a poor peasant girl, and some of the later emotional interchanges with his wife. Further, while the passages narrated in second-person singular, in the future tense, function with profound effect when they add the dimension of philosophical speculation, there are other times when the author was, in effect, locked in by his system of alternating points of view. Even though he may have wished to develop a sequence for primarily narrative reasons, it became necessary, at given points, because of the first-second-third pattern, to write this sequence in second-person singular and future tense. In general, the originality of this pattern, which is unlike that of any other contemporary modern novel, is striking and effective. But these qualities are achieved at the cost of imposing a sense of rigidity on the novel's structure.

On the whole, *The Death of Artemio Cruz* is not only technically more unified than Fuentes' first novel, but conceptually more coherent. It fuses existentialist themes of choice, individual responsibility, and guilt with a sophisticated economic interpretation of the sweep of Mexican history. While *Where the Air is Clear* gave evidence of an unlimited ambition in its effort to reflect all the crosscurrents operating on the Mexican scene, this later novel shows that the author is responsible not only to capture the spirit of the moment, but to impose upon this spirit some meaningful philosophical interpretation. As before, Fuentes poses important questions, but now he succeeds in defining the terms by which he feels they can be answered.

In this sense, Fuentes would seem to have maintained his *engagement* as a novelist, and determined to stretch to the fullest his capacity to wield his literary tools in order to communicate a valid statement.

6 | THE LITERARY CONTEXT: DYNAMISM AND DIVERSITY

THE FIFTEEN YEARS between the publication of *The Edge of the Storm* and *The Death of Artemio Cruz* represent in effect three literary generations—for generations come of age rapidly in the dizzy pace of post-Revolutionary Mexico. Each of the novelists already discussed was related in one way or another to his contemporaries. Each was reacting against, as well as influenced by, whatever was being published at the time. The literary art of fiction was expanding, proliferating, experimenting, moving forward. In general, there was a surge of dynamism, which was a logical function of the period. As the middle class asserted itself, publishing houses, both private and government subsidized, were able to flourish, and the number of educated readers increased each year. The result was a coming of age for the novel in Mexico.

Mexican fiction during these years is more varied in theme and focus than it had been earlier. Many novelists, as might be expected, follow the patterns of the 1930's, producing social-protest literature or works rooted in a simplistic evaluation of one or another phase of the Revolution. But the significant works, most of them dating from the late 1950's or early 1960's, began to establish two separate areas of thematic interest. There are those novels which, directly or indirectly, concern themselves with aspects of Mexican reality or problems of the individual in a societal context. By and large, they are influenced by the landmark authors.

There was also fiction which reflected a conscious effort to move directly toward universal themes and styles, tending away from social and national preoccupations. Entering the more abstract realms of philosophic or stylistic emphasis, these novels and short stories reduced somewhat the direct tie between literature and the major problems of the post-Revolution.

The two groupings are best discussed in terms of individual works rather than authors, for many writers—Arreola, Galindo, even Fuentes himself—produce narrative fiction varying greatly both in intent and technique.

Man in his Mexican Circumstance

Within the former grouping, which grapples with social relationships, one current is concerned with the unincorporated Indian presence. The *indigenista* novel of the 1950's and early 1960's searched in depth into Indian life, challenging the easy way in which the official nationalist establishment reaped the benefit of that heritage while disregarding the live peoples descended from those who produced it.

The theme of the downtrodden Indian is far from original in Mexican fiction. In the 1930's and 1940's, he was portrayed as the innocent victim of social injustice. In novels such as *El resplandor* and *El indio*, the latter replete with folkloric description of his way of life, authors like Mauricio Magdaleno and Gregorio López y Fuentes viewed him from outside his culture. In literary terms, this was largely an extension of the novel of the Revolution. Based on limited knowledge of the Indian, these works reflected the atmosphere of cultural nationalism and social reform of the period, and were aimed at the social conscience of middle-class urban readers.

In the following decade a new approach appeared. A series of novels and short stories attempted to present for the first time convincing Indian characters within the context of their own culture. These included: *Juan Pérez Jolote* (Ricardo Pozas, 1948), *El callado dolor de los tzotziles* (Ramón Rubín, 1949), *El diosero* (Francisco Rojas González, 1952), *Los hombres verdaderos* (Carlo Antonio Castro, 1959), *Benzulul* (Eraclio Zepeda, 1959), *La culebra tapó el río* (María Lombardo de Caso, 1962). All incorporated new anthropological conceptions, some included technical and stylistic innovations, but in general they achieved only modest literary success.

The world of *Oficio de tinieblas*[1] by Rosario Castellanos (1962) is considerably more complex. As in her two earlier works of fiction, *Balún Canán* (1957) and *Ciudad Real* (1960), the young author analytically lays bare the pattern of relations between Indian and *ladino* which influences all aspects and levels of life in traditional San

Cristóbal Las Casas, provincial center of highlands Chiapas, which had been the center of interest for most of the *indigenista* writers mentioned above.[2]

Preoccupied with the relationship between reality and myth, the work is constructed on two contrasting temporal planes. The action unfolds in a clearly historical framework —the period of the 1930's and just after, the epoch of Cárdenas and high point of the Mexican Revolution. In contrast, time for the Tzotzil Indian has the ahistorical quality of Indian legend. The opening paragraphs set the scene in San Juan Chamula, Tzotzil religious and political center, in terms of a Christianized myth, recounted in the language and images of the *Popol Vuh,* Mayan version of the creation. At the novel's end, the defeated Indian rebellion is synthesized, not in terms of battles won or lost, but in the form of newly fashioned myth. The narrator comments: "Naked, barely covered with rags, or with loinclothes of half-tanned leather, they have abolished the time that separated them from the past ages. There is no longer a before or today. Always. Always defeat and persecution."

The winds of reform, in the view of Rosario Castellanos, have been blocked from reaching the valley of San Cristóbal, as though the surrounding mountains had been erected to serve the prejudices of the controlling class of aristocratic *ladino* landholders. In effect, her novelistic interpretation indicts the Revolution for having succumbed to easy compromise at Indian expense, rather than do battle with the entrenched conservative forms, including the church, which conspire to retain centuries-old semifeudalism.

Unlike earlier views of the Indian, Castellanos' vision does not gloss over the negative effects of blind superstition, of ritualistic alcoholism, of daily, relentless humiliation. But there is also consistent affirmation, especially in the hope that springs up in each generation, and in the grim, almost subconscious determination to survive the buffetings of a hostile fate, all of which form part of the Tzotzil mentality.

Within this setting, Catalina Díaz Puiljá, the Tzotzil protagonist, emerges as a genuine literary character, a rarity in the Latin American novel, which almost never succeeds in portraying convincing Indian individuals. Transcending the folkloric and the regional, Catalina responds to motivations that are universal, as well as peculiar to local circumstances. Her basic problem is known to all women—sterility. But her response to the problem is conditioned by her own culture. She seeks power and gratification in her career as *ilol,* magic healer and interpreter of mystical Tzotzil beliefs.

The determinant in Indian life is the presence of the dominant society, presented in *Oficio de tinieblas* through a series of *ladino* characters of various social classes. Most interesting are the traditional landholder and his embittered wife, their unhappy daughter, a guilt-ridden bishop, and an ambitious priest. The most striking common characteristic in all these individuals is the degree to which their entire system of values has been corroded by a blend of hatred and fear of the Indians, upon whom they depend but whom they regard as inferior, distasteful, and essentially unredeemable. In a manner reminiscent of Faulkner, Castellanos dramatizes the human equation of prejudice: perpetration of injustice upon a vulnerable cultural group can be achieved only at the expense of corrupting and deforming the institutions—social, religious, political—of the exploiters.

Despite its regional focus and its concern for the inner

world of its Indian characters, the fiction of Castellanos and the other *indigenista* authors essentially constitutes a series of variations on the theme of anguish and despair. Both Indians and *ladinos* face tragedy or death, victims of an atmosphere of decadence and corrosion, which inevitably dominates the individual and renders him powerless. The world view partakes of international pessimism by implication, but strikes out at the same time against an Achilles' heel of modern Mexico—the widening gap between Indian and *mestizo*—exposing wounds which the Revolution did not heal and which continue to fester. The authors are not literary innovators, but their works develop a more penetrating view of this facet of Mexican reality. Fear, hatred, and prejudice are ecumenical values in man, but the form and substance which they acquire in contemporary Chiapas is unique, although comparable in important respects to Mississippi, Cuzco, or South Africa.

Another current of literature seeking to define Mexican reality harks back to *The Edge of the Storm* with its focus on a provincial town. New elaborations of this approach include *La comparsa* (Sergio Galindo, 1964), *Bramadero* (Tomás Mojarro, 1963), *La feria* (Juan José Arreola, 1963), and *Los recuerdos del porvenir* (Elena Garro, 1963).

In each case it is a *pueblo* which receives more rounded analysis than individuals. The authors have eschewed conventional character study in order to portray larger human composites. Similarly, there are thematic threads which run through all these works: a cynical view of bourgeois falsity, breakdown of morality, the pervasive and degrading influence of prostitution, the bitter tension between organized Catholicism and latter-day representatives of the Revolution.

La comparsa[3] by Sergio Galindo illuminates the personality of Jalapa, capital and university center of the state of Veracruz, in the cathartic explosion of the annual carnival. Traditional structure and plot development are avoided. The narration is conveyed in fragments of dialogue, interior monologues, and brief narrative passages. As his sparely sketched characters interact in diverse rapid-fire encounters, dramatic intensity accumulates to keep pace with the frenzy of Carnival.

Jalapa is defined in terms of its private idiosyncrasies —the Caribbean-oriented racial composition, the tense dialogue between university intelligentsia and the newly arrived middle class. But the author so disposes the town's individuality as to dramatize agonies which, far from being a regional phenomenon, have points of contact with the problems and frustrations of twentieth-century man. The quest for identity, the role of the individual in a modern society, the ambivalent role of sex as means of communication as well as degradation are familiar themes which unify the fragments of *La comparsa*.

Paz's motif of solitude and communion here finds new expression. Which is real, the year-round routine of inhibition, frustration, and bourgeois hypocrisy, or the momentary dynamism of the carnival, when conventional identities are cast off, and vehemence, exhibition, and extroversion reign supreme? A question posed by Galindo, but not answered.

Bramadero[4] by Tomás Mojarro, is a study of a town in shock. Set in backward Margil de Minas in rural Zacatecas circa 1940, it narrates the traumatic upheaval introduced by the arrival of a new highway. Attendant socio-economic changes jar the tenuous balance in Margil, a bitter equilibrium of antagonistic forces. On the one hand, there is the local clergy, submerged in pre-Revolutionary narrowness, capitalizing on primitive folk religiosity, counting on the support of the new post-Revolutionary bourgeoisie. Opposed to the clergy is the corrupt *cacique*, "el primer hombre," mouthing slogans about progress, technology, and civilization, but furiously engaged in self-enrichment and in the perverse harassment of the Church for motives more personal than ideological.

The real protagonist is the suffering Margil de Minas. Its complex social animosities, its *barrios* and churches, its "Museo del Cristo Vivo" which attracts visitors from miles around, its brand new brothel, fruit of the highway's progress—all these are defined more fully and subtly than any of the individual characters.

The literary merit of *Bramadero* depends upon style and language. The dominant note of cynicism and despair is conveyed by sensitive stylization—not reproduction—of provincial speech patterns. The novel is laden with images of the senses, many jarring and unpleasant. Odors of unwashed bodies, glare of unrelenting sun, penetrating din of church bells contribute to the distinctly sordid and grotesque tone by which Tomás Mojarro characterizes the ambivalent advent of progress in a Zacatecas town.

In *La feria*[5] by Juan José Arreola, it is a vision of the human dimensions of Zapotlán, a *pueblo* in southern Jalisco, which is portrayed sensitively. Here society is viewed with a perceptive skepticism tempered by a compassionate understanding of man's foibles.

Narrative substance derives from a gamut of subplots rooted in familiar themes of small-town existence: ludicrous emptiness of provincial intellectuals with their caricature of an *Ateneo*; the laboriously detailed struggle to force crops from a hostile soil; timeless Indian efforts to regain possession of their land, always frustrated; the middle class condemning but condoning prostitution; a Church perpetuating itself upon empty ritual and superstition.

Arreola's typical symbolism is suggested in the Zapotlán fair, the summation of the village yearly cycle. A giant fireworks display explodes, killing many bystanders, whose bodies are strewn in disorder, "like the dead on a false field of battle." A sorrowful finale indeed, to end the final paragraph in the story of the village efforts to survive another year's problems and hardships. Sensitive language underlines human contradiction. Bitter humor gives unity and freshness to a novel built upon material already treated by other authors.

A small town in southern Mexico is not only the ultimate protagonist, the final repository of experience for the characters, but also the narrator in *Los recuerdos del porvenir*[5] by Elena Garro. A traditional plot is elaborated with a new perspective—the prism of time through which the author views the microcosm of Ixtepec.

In constant opposition to the historical setting in the 1920's is the insistence by the *pueblo*-narrator that time is not valid. Since they have no control over time, the characters must confront the existential consciousness of death at every moment. The present is merely a function of past and future, of external forces such as tyranny and evil which control both man and his circumstance. In the prestructured trap of existence, memory can include the future, for the future is a reelaboration of the past. Although the marriage of realism and intuitive fantasy is not uniformly successful, the poetic, imaginative style of Elena Garro achieves a considerable degree of artistic cohesion.

In interpreting Mexico's recent historical past, this author is even more bitter than Mojarro, Galindo, Fuentes,

Castellanos, and others. "The Catholic Porfiristas and the atheistic revolutionaries together fashioned the tomb of the agrarian movement," states one character. Yet the novel projects beyond the elemental turmoil of Ixtepec to impart unquestionable literary merit to *Los recuerdos del porvenir.*

Besides the development of a town protagonist that receives more penetrating analysis than individual characters, there are thematic points of contact shared by all four of these novels. They continue the literature on provincial themes, a current which has sources deep in the nineteenth century. But modern values now emerge. Through the *pueblo* there is an attempt to grapple with the problems— social, spiritual, philosophical—of Mexico. But unlike the regionalist novel of the 1890's or the nationalistic novel of the 1930's, these works raise problems which are bound up with the dilemmas of the twentieth century. Their distinctive feature is that they explain these dilemmas not through a detailed analysis of introverted individuals, but rather through their characters' interaction within the social framework provided by their fellow townsmen.

A common and deeply rooted attitude in all these writers is their pessimism in regard to the Mexican Revolution —an attitude shared by most other Mexican novelists today. Elena Garro refers to the Revolution as betrayed. For Mojarro it is the Revolution corrupted; in Arreola, frustrated. Galindo's characters scarcely refer to it, except for slighting references to a venal political atmosphere. For them, it is an obsolete phenomenon which has outlived its usefulness.

A less representative current of the fiction committed to social commentary is one which rests frankly upon Marxist ideology. The outstanding writer in this group is José Revueltas, whose two most important novels, *El luto humano* (1943) *and Los errores* (1964) present themes of anguish and suffering in surroundings of sordid poverty. He is a portraitist of the lower depths, who brings to mind the acid brush of Orozco.

The later novel, *Los errores*,[7] is bitterly anti-Communist, despite its Marxist focus, reflecting the disillusionment of the recent period. In it, Revueltas creates literary worlds which at first exist autonomously, side by side. Gradually, and unfortunately not without straining, he interrelates the twin sets of characters until their fortunes interact and their destinies become inseparable. Of the two component plot lines, the more skilfully handled is that of a robbery and murder in Mexico City in the 1930's, in the jagged world of thieves, prostitutes, and grotesque dwarfs, with undertones of homosexuality and overtones of violence.

The second narrative sequence—the tactics of a Communist-led strike—presented problems which the author failed to solve in literary terms. Focusing on the moral-philosophical conflicts which confront Marxist idealists, Revueltas succumbs to the temptation of incorporating undigested political meanderings into the novel, presented as characters' thoughts. His subjectively bitter denunciation of the Stalin period undermines literary autonomy in a novel otherwise notable for the biting sharpness and power of its descriptive style.

Despite the distinctions of locale—urban, rural, or Indian village—all these novels have the social concerns of the nation in common. While most of them are not sociological per se, they may well be called social novels in the sense that they are rooted in the realities of the Mexican scene, uniformly critical, but at the same time committed to that nation. This tradition in fiction has produced a surprisingly large volume of valid literature, with considerable diversity, especially when compared to the literary output prior to *The Edge of the Storm.*

THE UNIVERSALIZERS

During the same period, however, there appeared many works that shunned any semblance of social preoccupation. These are works of fiction on universal themes, written by Mexicans, but which might just as well have appeared in Buenos Aires, Milan, Madrid, or Stuttgart.

Although for many years Juan José Arreola concentrated his creative writing in the area of the short story, his influence on the Mexican novel has been considerable. Arreola's short fiction since the early 1940's has been gathered in one volume entitled *Confabulario,* which in each edition since 1955 has been enlarged to include his subsequent stories.[8] A literary artisan, Arreola handcrafts his stories from thematic material of the most diverse sources: early French literature, medieval bestiaries, biblical parables, the Spanish classics, and the abstract propositions of modern science and technology. His technique shuns anecdotal narrative, focusing instead on illuminating human paradoxes by applying his fecund imagination to such wide subject matter. Thus, one story will recount an imagined incident in the life of a figure like Francois Villon, while others formulate a modern bestiary, in which the characteristics and behavior of the animals described point up the contradictions of modern society. Still others take the form of advertisements for imagined products, the features of which underline the modern penchant—emanating from United States factories—to rationalize existence in such a way that man's individuality is subordinated to the machine.

Clearly, Arreola's fiction stretches the traditional definition of the short story. The main ingredients he brings to the Mexican scene are his tone of satire with its altogether too rare element of humor, a deftness and economy of style, and a new, erudite range of literary subject matter. There are moments of Kafkian despair in Arreola, but they are counterbalanced by an underlying humanism which encases his exposition of the frailties of human nature in a context of sorrowful compassion.

Vincente Leñero's most important novel, *Los albañiles,*[9] had to win an important prize in Spain, the *Premio Biblioteca Breve,* before it could gain an audience in Mexico— proof perhaps that entering into new novelistic areas is not the easiest way to achieve recognition.

Los albañiles is a deceptive novel because its setting, a construction project in urban Mexico City, and its characters, members of the working class, give a first impression of a novel of social orientation. But the harsh, earthy language of the brick masons, which effectively communicates the abrasive quality of their personal relations, also serves another purpose. It points up the various forms of degradation in modern urban life and, in so doing, establishes the fact that there is more than one character with sufficient motivation to have committed the murder which is the novel's "inciting incident."

Narrative structure, constantly shifting from one point of view to another, and from interior monologue with overtones of fantasy to conventional third-person accounts, channels the reader's interest away from easy social and criminological analysis to more complex questions. Ultimately, beneath the study of the degradation which is exemplified in distorted sexual relationships, lies an examination of philosophical problems, such as the relativity of guilt, the ethics of justice, and the impossibility of knowing pure truth.

The basic puzzles with which the author confounds the reader make it clear that the Mexican setting, sharply delineated as it is, is merely the vehicle for philosophic examination of universal problems inherent in modern society. *Los albañiles,* remarkably sure in style and sophisticated in its narrative structure, takes the post-Revolution for granted and assumes that literature must explore the limitations of human nature, human knowledge, and morality.

Fuentes, himself, has explored thematic areas at the opposite pole from *The Death of Artemio Cruz.* In *Aura* (1962),[10] he treats the eternal conflict between illusion and reality. The novella, hardly longer than a short story, concerns a young historian who takes employment with an incredibly ancient woman to edit the papers of her long deceased husband. Felipe becomes increasingly involved with the niece, Aura, who, it becomes clear, is a projection of the old woman herself.

Descriptive style, in consonance with the romantic traditions of the Gothic tale, establishes in lush fullness an atmosphere compounded of mystery and decay, isolated from the pulsations of modern Mexico City in which the story is set. Reinforcing the tenuousness of reality are ambiguity of language, dual meaning, and conceptual antithesis, as the protagonist struggles in vain to place in some logical order the paradoxes he experiences.

A clue to the attitude toward life which underlies *Aura* can be found in a particular motif which appears on three distinct occasions—superimposition. It first occurs as Felipe looks for the house of Señora Consuelo, in the architectural juxtaposition of old and new. The motif next appears in a nightmare of Felipe, when Aura laughs at him with the old lady's teeth superimposed on her own. Finally, Felipe sees his own image in the dead General's photograph.

The image of false or temporary characteristics super-imposed on a more lasting, permanent construction is one index of the value which Fuentes assigns to time and historical progression. The thrust of the narration is unlike that of *Where the Air is Clear,* which examines a tenuous equilibrium between past and present. In the novella, the figure of Aura comes to incarnate the essential instability of a present dominated by preexisting forms and character-istics—a present which is merely a figment of the past.

In this world where reality proves false, disintegrating before the very eyes of the protagonist, the stature of man is diminished, for he commands no resources to cope with the mysterious forces which intrude on his consciousness and on his life: the force of the past, a monster whose ten-tacles reach into present-day existence; the force of the black arts, expressed in distorted religious symbols which generate a power superior to that of the intellect. His only recourse is his senses, and ultimately they betray him.

Significantly, Felipe is an historian, trained in the logic of ordering known facts into coherent larger expres-sions about man across time. But rationalism has little place in the world of Señora Consuelo, which embodies the state-ment by Jules Michelet introducing the novel: "Man hunts and struggles. Woman intrigues and dreams; she is the mother of fantasy, the mother of the gods. She has second sight, the wings that enable her to fly to the infinite of desire and imagination. . . . The gods are like men: they are born and they die on a woman's breast . . . ."[11]

In the cosmos of *Aura* dark predominates over light, the irrational conquers the rational, the subjective processes of the mind prove superior to objective time and place, man's futile struggle with circumstance is overwhelmed in the deeper fantasy symbolically projected by woman. Fuentes finds the roots of myth in European-Christian culture: the black Christ, analogy between sexual intercourse and Christian communion, and medieval Gothic symbols and atmosphere. Interestingly, the presence of the Indian heritage is not evident.

Aura is certainly not an attempt to explore the national consciousness, despite the setting and the flashbacks with historical reference. Environment is incidental to exploration of the irrational component of life where, unlike the world of Artemio Cruz, man is prisoner of the occult forces of irreality, fantasy, and myth.

Fuentes stated, in comparing *Aura* and *The Death of Artemio Cruz,* that he was precisely concerned with capturing the duality in human existence, in which man at moments faces annihilation and terror, and at other moments can strive for personal liberty. For one side of the coin, he had relied on the illumination of historical analysis. For the darker side, he had depended upon the multi-layered suggestivity of literary style.[12] In this sense, these two very different works complement each other.

On the other hand, in speaking of *Aura,* Fuentes stated that even a subjective and phantasmagoric conception of reality implies a view of the external world. In a comment that would seem almost designed to extend Fuentes' statement, the Uruguayan critic, Rodríguez Monegal observed: ". . . that woman who achieves through a powerful effort of the will the projection of a visible form of her youth which ensnares the protagonist . . . compelling him to relive with her (or with her double) a past which is dead—that woman symbolizes the reconstruction of the Mexico of the old days of privilege upon the structure of today's modern and inso-

lent Mexico."[13] To state it somewhat differently: just as
Aura is merely an ephemeral, momentary creation whose
beauty conceals the permanent features of the past, so today's facade (of Mexico, but not exclusively so) is in fact
an appealing but fragile device built upon reactionary, semifeudal patterns of earlier history.

A fair general statement would be that the conceptual
basis of *Aura* is rooted in the eternal mysteries which overcome man. Its stylistic lineage can be traced in literary pa-
ternity to Edgar Allan Poe and the English Gothic novel.
Clearly this novella, despite the indirect vision it projects of
the Mexican experience, is more suggestive of European and
American heritage than of its Mexican forebears.

Whether the novel of the past two decades was searching out Mexican identity, testifying to the continued anguish
of the Indian, exposing social sores in town or city, or
whether, on the other hand, it turned inward to extract from
self the basic verities, the fact remains that a literary movement, not just a few outstanding authors, was producing
writing which was new. The proliferation of roads is in itself
an indication of vigor.

This has become increasingly clear from the latter part
of the 1950's until the present. In a sense, Carlos Fuentes
was the most fortunate of the landmark authors, in that the
literary climate prevailing during his formative years as a
novelist was so dynamic. Not only were Yáñez, Rulfo, and
Arreola well established, but a whole new generation of his
contemporaries—Galindo, Castellanos, Garro, Mojarro, and
others—were competing for the attention of the public, and
expanding reading interests in several directions at once.

Essentially these latter years make evident an increasing number of authors concerned with probing for new perspectives of viewing Mexican reality, just as Yáñez, Rulfo,

and Fuentes did. They also reveal a new strain of fiction, in which imagination, individual expression, even fantasy are prime values, thus sowing the seeds for the kind of preoccupation shared by many of today's rising young writers.

There is no doubt that the landmark novels made an unprecedented contribution to a novelistic tradition in which the writer seeks a commitment to both society and art. It is also equally true that influences were reciprocal and that in varying degrees these outstanding authors drew sustenance and stimulation from the literary context in which they worked.

7 | FRUITS OF THE STORM

IT WOULD BE RASH in the productive present to predict a future direction for the Mexican novel, especially when diverse currents have capable exponents, and when some of the most talented writers seem bent on traveling down more than one path.

But it is safe to say that a major hurdle has been surmounted. A valid heritage has been established in the genre, with its own vision and enough enrichment to provide a solid pedestal upon which to build that future. To a large extent the landmark novels, *The Edge of the Storm, Pedro Páramo, Where the Air is Clear,* and *The Death of Artemio Cruz* have built it.

Each of the three authors of these works performed the constructive if traditional role of critical conscience of the nation. Because they insisted on artistic autonomy, their works generate a mirror-image which delves beneath the superficial features of the society to enter into the domain which Unamuno has called "intra-historia," the spiritual life of the nation.

Their focus is man. His problems are his own, they say, either self-created or his own alone to solve or to bear. Thus they differ with their predecessors' views, based on a variety of determinisms which subordinated the individual to some higher order, such as nature, abstract social institutions, or God. Yáñez examines the explosive tension resulting when rigid social and moral norms are imposed on a *pueblo* inhabited by complex individuals, each with his own internal dynamics and his own personality. Rulfo's archetypal protagonist lives a timeless anguish rooted in his sin and guilt. And the dying moments of Artemio Cruz are a desperate attempt to come to grips with conscience, reliving personal crises which shaped the destiny of a character memorable both as an individual and as a representative of a larger social unit. The forest of Mexico is present in these works, but amplitude of focus permits detailed views of the individual trees in the foreground.

From Yáñez' analytical criticism to Rulfo's unmitigated despair, there is commitment to Mexico, but not endorsement. In one or another, the psychology of Freud and Jung, the philosophy of Marx and Sartre, the formulations of Frazer and Graves concerning mythology have been taken into account. Within the framework of a personal vision, each novel measures Mexico's dilemmas, with all their peculiarities, in terms which render them comparable to those of modern man. Yáñez, Rulfo, and Fuentes challenge the traditional dichotomy between national and universal, and, to a significant extent, they succeed in solving it.

Because expression of the inner image required the shaping of language to conform to the particular thematic

material, each author explored a unique style, ranging from
the baroque patterns of Yáñez to the distilled lyricism of
Rulfo and the metaphoric ambiguity of Fuentes, each with
its own strengths and limitations. The ringing cadences of
The Edge of the Storm at times become tedious and sentimental. The inventive structure in which the stylized phrases
of *Pedro Páramo* are encased is so obscure that meanings
are inaccessible at first reading, while words and images
pour from Fuentes' pen in such profusion that he sometimes
loses control. Excesses notwithstanding, each author forges
a successful personal style.

Narrative techniques from abroad were employed, not
primarily in imitation of world esteemed models, but corresponding to inner mandates. The interior monologues of
Yáñez were not merely a technical innovation, but were essential to his psychological probing. Rulfo's denial of omniscience decreed a structure in which the reader participates in ordering events. His flight from historical causality
led him to the world of Frazer, the perspective of death
dictating the creation of myth. Fuentes, more than any,
shopped abroad for whatever he felt could extend his vision.
At times undigested, as in the Dos Passos-like headlines in
Where the Air is Clear, his borrowings were more often
organic to his conception. In *The Death of Artemio Cruz*
the alter-ego narration in the future tense makes possible
the existentialist reliving of the protagonist's crucial choices.
An innovative technique carries forward that which had
been imported. The Mexican novel had reached enough
maturity and self-confidence so that it could emulate without
echoing. Standing on its own merits, it could assimilate
whatever was serviceable from others.

The major novels are ambitious works, both in content
and in form. None achieves completely the task it sets, but

their authors share the conviction that in order to express subtle and profound meaning, the novel must be true to itself.

With so much accomplished, it is not surprising that a reaction has set in, at least against those aspects of the novel which tie each of them to a national orientation. The very achievements of Yáñez, Fuentes, and Rulfo make it difficult for new writers to venture into their territory without being labeled forthwith as derivative or imitative.

In the summer of 1965, Fuentes offered an explanation of the new trends toward treatment of highly personal or basically abstract themes. It was logical, he said, to expect a reaction against the excesses of cultural nationalism. The advent of the Revolution, he observed, gave rise to a new set of Mexican themes and techniques which reached their synthesis in such mural painters as Tamayo, poets like Paz, and the novelists, Yáñez and Rulfo. But there followed a sterile period of degeneration into what he called "auto-caricature," a hardening into established patterns. The new artists rebel against what have now become formulae, refusing, as Fuentes stated, to awaken each morning asking themselves, "What does it mean to be Mexican?"; "Am I the result of the dramatic clash between two races?"; "What is the true meaning of the cactus?"[1]

Furthermore, as Rosario Castellanos pointed out, many young writers have little concern or respect for their predecessors. It has been the custom throughout Mexican literature for each new generation to ignore tradition and insist on discovering the Mediterranean for itself. "We always begin from zero, and finish by discovering what was already known."[2]

The development of a flourishing middle class in Mexico has made inevitable the increased adoption of norms and goals of the middle class the world over. By contrast, the role of the intellectual as spokesman for the nation, as diagnostician of the national ills, has decreased, as Carlos Fuentes pointed out in his interview with Luis Harss and Barbara Dohmann. The young writer, no longer anticipating that his pen will have a profound impact upon his country, is more prone to the problems of alienation experienced by his colleagues in the overdeveloped capitalist countries of the West.[3]

Indeed, the new success of the novel, together with the vastly increased government commitment to education and to all aspects of culture, have already given rise to a series of literary and cultural institutions which may subtly affect the Mexican penchant for deep-rooted, national critical analysis—by channeling it into other directions or by placing a premium on other values. Increasing government influence has been felt in recent years in the *Centro Mexicano de Escritores,* in national writers' groups, in the leadership of the theoretically autonomous National University, and in the distinguished publishing house, Fondo de Cultura Económica.

In art, the problem of institutionalization was raised as early as 1955 by José Luis Cuevas. His well-known essay in the *Evergreen Review,* tendentious and overly bitter though it may have been in its attack against the "cactus curtain," described how the government establishment, ranging from critics to scholarship committees, tended to promote official style and themes, preventing young artists from being innovative and open to influences from abroad.[4]

Paradoxically, today's dominant literary hierarchy seems to favor cosmopolitanism, stressing abstraction and concern for novelistic form per se, or the particular complexities of interpersonal relationships, most frequently exemplified in sexual matters or adolescent troubles in a modern urban metropolis—the very subjectivity scorned by officialdom in other media. The novel is the art form which has been most penetratingly critical of the status quo, which may account for encouragement of new themes and attitudes.

Fuentes himself feels that a writer, like any other citizen, has the civic responsibility of concern for the world around him. He feels the need to be free to develop his own strain of heterodox, antidogmatic thinking. A power structure, he says, should always have before it a mirror—the novel—at times affirming, at times negating its profile.[5] But as an artist he is in as much a state of flux as the Mexican novel as a whole, searching for ideological bearings, testing new themes, and rejecting the direction of his own past work.

The current generation which is freeing itself from a national preoccupation which it considers stale, inevitably will encounter new pitfalls. Imitation of international models is as insidious as repeating local products. If new writers assume, says Fuentes, that analysing problems of the modern bourgeoisie entitles them to an automatic passport to universality, they will slip into the sterility of *"tele-novelas."*[6]

Product of cosmopolitan Mexico City, cut off from an unchanging rural hinterland, the younger writer may feel himself more closely akin to his contemporaries in Berlin, Paris, and Chicago than to the realities and traditions of Mexico and its literature. Rather than turn to Rulfo and Fuentes for inspiration, he is likely to look to Pavese, Salinger, or Robbe-Grillet. The psychological narrative of alienated individuals hopelessly striving for communication in a heartlessly modernized society may appear more real to him than the betrayal of a revolution long since converted into myth.

On the other hand, Mexico City is not the capital of Germany, France, or the United States. An interesting phenomenon of the past few years has been the increasing amount of contact and mutual identification between many of the outstanding writers of Latin America—indicating that a possible middle ground between national preoccupation and full-blown cosmopolitanism may be a new Latin American consciousness.

Examples of this new development are many. In preparation for the Congress of Latin American Writers, held in Mexico in the spring of 1967, Juan Rulfo visited the leading capitals of South America, contacting writers and discussing mutual interests. The Congress was attended by outstanding figures in the novel such as Miguel Angel Asturias, Mario Benedetti, and Alejo Carpentier (although many of the younger Mexican writers stayed away out of resentment against the Mexican government's attempt to control the content of the sessions through several older authors whose primary public role is more that of government functionary).

A different type of mutual contact and stimulation has been the constant interchange of personal visits, letters, and fragments of manuscripts between writers such as Fuentes and Mario Vargas Llosa of Peru, Alejo Carpentier of Cuba, Julio Cortázar of Argentina, José Donoso of Chile, and Gabriel García Márquez of Colombia. Most of these writers have been influenced by Carpentier's formulations on the Latin American novel, its possibilities and peculiarities, embodied in the term "lo real-maravilloso" (magical realism).[7] Similarly, all have read the brilliant Fuentes article of several years ago on the achievements of the new generation of novelists.[8] Evidence that there is a conscious effort to "Latin-Americanize" the novel is the striking fact that in the recent García Márquez novel, *Cien años de soledad*,[9] the author has actually included references in the lives of his characters to characters from *The Death of Artemio Cruz* and *Rayuela (Hopscotch)*, by the Argentine Julio Cortázar—thus setting up an organic contact between his own novelistic world and that of authors from other countries.

A most important source of Latin American consciousness has been the fact that for almost a decade, Cuba has constituted for many established and budding writers a literary epicenter. From it has emanated the journal, *Casa de las Américas*, in which a number of indispensable studies have appeared. Most significant has been the series of annual prize competitions, in the novel as well as other genres, in which many young writers have entered their works for the first time in international competition. A large number of authors and critics have also attended the competitions as members of the selection juries.

This phenomenon is difficult to estimate in the rarefied political atmosphere of the United States, in which Castroism is construed as anathema to cultural freedom. In point of fact, most of the Mexican writers who have visited Cuba and participated in its literary competitions are precisely the writers who in Mexico produce the most avant-garde, universally oriented literature. Further, many have also enjoyed visits and lecture tours in the United States. Examples are Emilio Carballido, Juan José Arreola, and Juan García Ponce. This willingness to identify publicly with Cuba is a complex manifestation of an instinctive desire in many writers to make common cause with the left, a need to demonstrate public independence, and, at the same time, a new understanding that there is a possible community of interest between the novelists of underdeveloped Latin America which is different from all the lessons to be learned and the inspiration to be absorbed in Paris and Rome.

In Mexico, the controversy still rages, as it has for generations, as to whether the writer should concern himself with the particular characteristics of his nationality, whether the sights and sounds or the problems and issues or the psychological shadings, but the terms of the debate have changed. The writers no longer congregate in seminars in the Palace of Fine Arts, like Manuel Zamacona in *Where the Air is Clear,* to consider whether that which is most national is, at the same time, most universal. The word nationalism is now anathema in the writing profession. The term revolution is more likely to refer to Cuba's than to the one that set Mexico aflame in 1910, and still glowed as a beacon of hope three decades later. Even the disillusionment in its aftermath has been stated and restated until, to many writers today, it may seem like a fruitless occupation.

Yet, on the other hand, Zamacona's lament, "many formulas, no books," is now far from true. The man who created him—Carlos Fuentes—as well as Rulfo and Yáñez, helped generate the outpouring of the written word of the past two decades. If all of it does not match up to the "landmark" novels, most of it does justice to them. The themes are varied, the styles inventive, the writers committed to their art—all essential in the development of a literature, which is what is taking place in Mexico today. If it cannot be called a "national" literature, and if in fact the term would be denied hotly by many of its practitioners, it is partly because such boundaries are less valid today, especially among those who are producing the books.

It is impossible to foresee precisely a new direction. Talent is too unpredictable a commodity, the literary and social scenes too complex. But artists seldom arise without a base, even if much creative energy is consumed in overthrowing what has gone before. Yáñez, Rulfo, and Fuentes opened new vistas in order to reject and transcend the novel of the Revolution, while the present mood may in turn react against these same innovators.

The landmark novels achieved a balance in the crucial post-Revolutionary confrontation between national preoccupation and universal values. The pendulum of the novel seeks its equilibrium between the social and the personal, the historical and the mythical, and between commitment and objectivity, realism and estheticism. A particular direction is easier to point out when that pendulum is farthest from midpoint, but both art and life have a way of pulling it back down to center. It is in that rich pivotal area that the landmark novels can be placed.

NOTES

NOTE TO PREFACE

1. (Austin: University of Texas Press, 1966).

NOTES TO CHAPTER I

1. Samuel Ramos, *El perfil del hombre y la cultura en México*, 2nd ed., (México: Editorial Robredo, 1938).

2. Frank Dauster, *Breve historia de la poesía mexicana* (México: Ediciones de Andrea, 1956), p. 104. Translation by J. Sommers, as are all subsequent translated passages from texts in Spanish, unless otherwise indicated.

3. Antonio Castro Leal, ed. *La Novela de la Revolución Mexicana* (México: Aguilar, 1960), I, xvii.

4. A descriptive account of the polemic in Mexico which focused popular and critical attention on *Los de abajo* is contained in John E. Englekirk's "The Discovery of *Los de abajo* by Mariano Azuela," *Hispania*, XVIII (1935), 53-62.

5. Luis Leal, *Mariano Azuela, Vida y Obra* (México: Ediciones de Andrea, 1961), p. 48.

6. Mariano Azuela, *Los de abajo*, Colección Popular (México: Fondo de Cultura Económica, 1960), p. 72. All subsequent references will be to this edition, and will appear in the text. Translations are my own, though I have often referred to the English translation, entitled *The Underdogs*, tr. E. Munguía, Jr. (New York: Brentano's, 1929).

7. Enrique Anderson Imbert, *Historia de la literatura hispanoamericana*, 3rd ed. (México: Fondo de Cultura Económica, 1961), I, 418.

8. The best known work of Guzmán, *El águila y la serpiente (The Eagle and the Serpent)*, is not treated here because although it influ-

enced the course of the novel of the Revolution, it is in reality not a novel but semifictionalized biography, imaginatively and imagefully written.

9. Martín Luis Guzmán, *La sombra del caudillo* in Antonio Castro Leal, ed., *op. cit.*, p. 452. All subsequent references will be to this edition and will appear in the text.

10. Mauricio Magdaleno, *El resplandor* (México: Ediciones Botas, 1937).

11. José Luis Martínez, *Literatura mexicana, Siglo XX* (México: Antigua Librería Robredo, 1949), I, 46.

12. Mauricio Magdaleno, *Sunburst*, tr. Anita Brenner (New York: Viking, 1944), p. 6.

13. The term nationalism as used here is not in the sense of its possible xenophobic or aggressive manifestations, but in accordance with the general definition of Hans Kohn: "Nationalism is a state of mind, permeating the large majority of a people and claiming to permeate all its members; it recognizes the nation-state as the ideal form of political organization and the nationality as the source of all creative cultural energy and of economic well-being. The supreme loyalty of man is therefore due to his nationality, as his own life is supposedly rooted in and made possible by its welfare." Hans Kohn, *The Idea of Nationalism* (New York: Macmillan, 1960), p. 16.

14. John Brushwood and José Rojas Garcidueñas, *Breve historia de la novela mexicana* (México: Ediciones de Andrea, 1959), p. 132.

15. Azuela was born in 1873, Guzmán in 1887, and Magdaleno in 1906.

Notes to Chapter II

1. Agustín Yáñez, *Al filo del agua* (México: Editorial Porrúa, 1955), pp. 8-9. All subsequent references will be to the second edition, dated 1955, and will appear in the text. Translations frequently, but never completely, rely upon the edition in English, *The Edge of the Storm*, tr. Ethel Brinton (Austin: University of Texas Press, 1963).

2. Elaine Haddad, "The Structure of *Al filo del agua*," *Hispania*, XLVII (Sept. 1964), 523.

3. One example of this view is José Rojas Garcidueñas, "Notas sobre tres novelas mexicanas," *Anales del Instituto de Investigaciones Estéticas*, IV, 16 (1948), 16, who states that the novel actually begins on page 175.

4. This example was chosen intentionally because it has evoked comments with which I disagree. Manuel Pedro González, *Trayectoria de la novela en México* (México: Ediciones Botas, 1951), pp. 332-333, cites essentially the same lines. He then states, "This is undeniably beautiful and rhythmic, but in prose one cannot abuse such a technique without producing a sensation of monotony and fatigue." Elaine Haddad, "The Structure of *Al filo del agua*," pp. 525-526, cites a briefer fragment of the same passage and comments, "Whereas the density of the author's prose has been and will continue to be effective in establishing the heaviness of the town, it is not convincing in such passages. There is a danger in talking too much about emotion." This particular example of prose is effective, I believe, because it blends stylistic elaboration, rhythmical quality, and meaningful religious symbols to achieve thematic depth. On the other hand, subsequent parts of the same chapter do fall into exaggeration and sentimentality because of technical weaknesses, as indicated below.

5. *La imagen en el espejo* (Mexico: U.N.A.M., 1965), p. 147.

6. "Otra vez *Al filo del agua*," *Universidad de México*, XVI (Nov. 1961), 21-22.

7. "Novelística de Agustín Yáñez," *Memoria del Octavo Congreso del Instituto Internacional de Literatura Iberoamericana* (México: Editorial Cultura, 1961), p. 229.

8. "The Structure of *Al filo del agua*," p. 527.

9. In a subsequent novel, *La creación* (México: Fondo de Cultura Económica, 1959) Yáñez follows the careers of several characters from *Al filo del agua* during the years of the Revolution. But to introduce evidence from this other (and incidentally much less successful) novel would be to deny the wholeness of the world view in the work under discussion.

10. As quoted in an interview with Emmanuel Carballo, in Carballo's book, *Diecinueve protagonistas de la literatura mexicana del siglo XX* (México: Empresas Editoriales, S.A., 1965), p. 291.

11. "Novela y provincia: Agustín Yáñez," *México en la Cultura (Novedades)*, Sept. 4, 1961, p. 3.

NOTES TO CHAPTER III

1. Juan Rulfo, *Pedro Páramo* (México: Fondo de Cultura Económica, 1955), p. 7. All subsequent references will be to the fifth edition, dated 1964, and will appear in the text. Translations rely

heavily, but never completely, upon the edition in English, *Pedro Páramo*, tr. Lysander Kemp (New York: Grove Press, 1959).

2. One critic, Hugo Rodríguez-Alcalá, *El Arte de Juan Rulfo* (México: Instituto Nacional de Bellas Artes), pp. 95-103, expands on this notion of contrast, finding a duality in the novel's setting: Comala as Inferno, Comala as Paradise.

3. The fatalism implicit in this technique is discussed by James East Irby, *La influencia de William Faulkner en cuatro narradores hispanoamericanos* (México: Universidad Nacional Autónoma de México, 1956). Irby finds Faulknerian influence in chaotic structure, the use of a witness narrator, fatalistic reviewing of the past, and the selection of an archaic, decadent segment of society upon which to base a literary opus.

4. "Realidad y estilo de Juan Rulfo," *Revista Mexicana de Literatura*, I, 1 (1955), 72. This excellent early study also examines fatalism in *Pedro Páramo* and the contrast between the laconic, apparently objective narration and an ultimately subjective world view, based on distortion of the traditional time-place framework of reality.

5. "Trayectoria novelística de Agustín Yáñez," *Memoria del Sexto Congreso del Instituto Internacional de Literatura Iberoamericana* (México: Imprenta Universitaria, 1954), p. 240.

6. Concerning the symbolic value of the name "Páramo," Hugo Rodríguez-Alcalá cited a letter by Robert Mead, Jr. to *The New York Times Book Review*, August 9, 1959, p. 17. Professor Mead stated, "Selden Rodman's perceptive review of Juan Rulfo's *Pedro Páramo*, in which he quite properly emphasizes the symbolism of the novel, would have been even more meaningful if he had pointed out that 'Páramo' means desert or barren land in Spanish. For, despite the struggles of Rulfo's characters, their lives are unresolved and they exist, dead or alive, in a barren world of wasted effort."

7. "Sartoris, par William Faulkner," *Nouvelle revue française*, L, 293 (Feb. 1938), 324 (translation my own). This quotation was also cited by James East Irby.

8. The necessity of reader participation as coauthor is discussed by Mariana Frenk, *"Pedro Páramo," Universidad de México*, XV, 11 (July 1961), 19.

9. "Realidad y estilo de Juan Rulfo," p. 81.

10. *Ibid.*, p. 85.

11. Carlos Fuentes, "La nueva novela latinoamericana," *La Cultura en México*, No. 128, supplement to *Siempre!*, July 29, 1964, p. 3.

12. "Notes on the Study of Myth," *Partisan Review*, XIII, 3 (Summer 1946), 342-343.

13. *Ibid.*, p. 344.
14. *El Arte de Juan Rulfo,* p. 132-135.

NOTES TO CHAPTER IV

1. For a critical summary of Fuentes' literary production, see Robert Mead, "Carlos Fuentes, Mexico's Angry Novelist," *Books Abroad,* XXXVIII (Autumn 1964), 380-382. Professor Mead has expanded and updated this study in "Carlos Fuentes, Airado Novelista Mexicano," *Hispania,* L, 2 (1967), 229-235.

2. Carlos Fuentes, *La región más transparente* (México: Fondo de Cultura Económica, 1958). All subsequent references will be to the third edition, dated 1960, and will appear in the text. Translations rely somewhat on the edition in English, *Where The Air Is Clear,* tr. Sam Hileman (New York: Obolensky, 1960).

3. "Psychological-Literary Techniques in Representative Contemporary Novels of Mexico," Ph.D. Diss., University of Maryland, 1965, p. 371.

4. *Ibid.*, p. 344.

5. This typographical format copies the original as closely as possible in an attempt to show the degree of experimentation employed in these passages.

6. Samuel O'Neill, "Psychological-Literary Techniques," p. 408.

7. *Ibid.*, p. 376.

8. In a tape-recorded interview at his home in August, 1965, Fuentes told me: "I feel I have been deeply influenced by William Faulkner. I think Faulkner, of the American writers, is the closest to us because he is the only novelist of defeat, in a country that basically has been a nation of optimism and success. Furthermore, he is the only baroque writer in the U.S. Once, Alejo Carpentier told me, as we walked in the streets of Havana, that we Latin Americans are baroque because *el barroco* is a way of seeking truth. When there are established truths, accepted by all, one can be classical. When there is no stable truth, we have to be baroque." (Translation my own.) Other ideas he expressed in this conversation were presented in my article, "The Present Moment in the Mexican Novel," *Books Abroad,* XL (Summer 1966), 261-266.

9. "El mundo mágico de Carlos Fuentes," *Número* (Montevideo), I, 2 (1963), 147.

10. *Into The Mainstream: Conversations with Latin-American Writers* (New York: Harper & Row, 1967), pp. 293-294.

11. Octavio Paz, *El laberinto de la soledad* (México: Ediciones Cuadernos Americanos, 1950). The quotations below are taken directly from the excellent English translation, *The Labyrinth of Solitude*, tr. Lysander Kemp (New York: Grove Press, 1961).

12. *The Labyrinth*, p. 20.

13. *Ibid.*, p. 144.

14. *Ibid.*, p. 11.

15. *Ibid.*, p. 89.

16. *Ibid.*, p. 96.

17. *Ibid.*, pp. 146-147.

18. *Ibid.*, p. 49.

19. *Ibid.*, p. 25.

20. *Ibid.*, pp. 71-72.

21. *Ibid.*, p. 210.

22. *Ibid.*, p. 211.

23. One of the official slogans of the government party, the PRI. The implication is that the Revolution has traveled a unique path, uninfluenced by outside ideologies or examples, and has achieved great progress.

24. *The Labyrinth*, p. 191.

NOTE TO CHAPTER V

1. Carlos Fuentes, *La muerte de Artemio Cruz* (México: Fondo de Cultura Económica, 1962). All subsequent references are to this first edition, and appear in the text. Translations are my own. The edition in English is entitled *The Death of Artemio Cruz*, tr. Sam Hileman (New York: Farrar, Straus, 1964).

NOTES TO CHAPTER VI

1. (México: Joaquín Mortiz, 1962). References below are to this edition and are in the text.

2. A more detailed study of this *indigenista* literature centered in Chiapas can be found in my article, "El ciclo de Chiapas: nueva corriente literaria," *Cuadernos Americanos*, CXXXIII, 2 (1964), 246-261.

3. (México: Joaquín Mortiz, 1964).

4. (México: Fondo de Cultura Económica, 1963).

5. (México: Joaquín Mortiz, 1963).

6. (México: Joaquín Mortiz, 1963).

7. (México: Fondo de Cultura Económica, 1964).

8. The most recent version is entitled *Confabulario Total (1941-1946)* (México: Fondo de Cultura Económica, 1962). The version in English bears the same title, *Confabulario*, tr. George Schade (Austin: University of Texas Press, 1964).

9. (Barcelona: Seix Barral, 1964).

10. (México: Era, 1962). The English translation has the same title, *Aura*, tr. Lysander Kemp (New York: Farrar, Straus & Giroux, 1965).

11. *Ibid.*, p. 7. Translation my own.

12. Joseph Sommers, "The Present Moment in the Mexican Novel," *Books Abroad*, XL (Summer 1966), 262.

13. "El mundo mágico de Carlos Fuentes," pp. 154-155. (Translation my own).

Notes to Chapter VII

1. Sommers, "The Present Moment in the Mexican Novel," p. 262.

2. *Ibid.*, p. 265.

3. *Into the Mainstream*, pp. 305-306.

4. "The Cactus Curtain," *Evergreen Review*, II (Winter 1959), 111-120.

5. "The Present Moment in the Mexican Novel," p. 263.

6. *Ibid.*, pp. 262-263.

7. Several of Carpentier's writings on the Latin American novel were published in the collection of his essays *Tientos y diferencias* (México: U.N.A.M. 1964).

8. "La nueva novela latinoamericana," *La Cultura en México*, No. 128, supplement to *Siempre!*, July 29, 1964, pp. 2-7 and 14-16.

9. (Buenos Aires: Editorial Sudamericana, 1967).

SELECTED BIBLIOGRAPHY

GENERAL STUDIES OF THE TWENTIETH-CENTURY
MEXICAN NOVEL

Alegría, Fernando. *Historia de la novela hispanoamericana.*
México: Ediciones de Andrea, 1965.

Brushwood, John S. *Mexico in its Novel.* Austin: University of
Texas Press, 1966.

Campos, Julieta. "La novela mexicana después de 1940," in her
La imagen en el espejo. México: U.N.A.M., 1965.

Carballo, Emmanuel. "Del costumbrismo al realismo crítico,"
Espiral (Bogotá), No. 91 (June 1964), 7-32.

—————. *Diecinueve protagonistas de la literatura mexicana
del siglo XX.* México: Empresas Editoriales, 1965.

Carter, Boyd G. "The Mexican novel at mid-century," *Prairie
Schooner,* XXVIII, 2 (Summer 1954), 143-156.

Castellanos, Rosario. "La novela mexicana contemporánea y su
valor testimonial," *Hispania,* XLVII, 2 (May 1964), 223-
230.

González, Manuel Pedro. *Trayectoria de la novela en México.*
México: Botas, 1951.

Leal, Luis. "Contemporary Mexican Literature: A Mirror of
Social Change," *Arizona Quarterly,* XVIII (Autumn
1962), 197-207.

Magaña Esquivel, Antonio. *La novela de la Revolución*. México: Instituto Nacional de Estudios Históricos de la Revolución Mexicana, 1964.

Martínez, José Luis. *Problemas literarios*. México: Obregón, S.A., 1955.

Morton, F. Rand. *Los novelistas de la Revolución mexicana*. México: n.p., 1949.

Los narradores ante el público. México: Joaquín Mortiz, 1966.

Ocampo de Gómez, Aurora Maura. *Literatura mexicana contemporánea: Biobibliografía crítica*. México: n.p., 1965.

Rosaldo, Renato. "A Decade of Mexican Literature: 1950-1960," *Arizona Quarterly*, XVI (Winter 1960), 319-331.

Sainz, Gustavo. "Diez años de literatura mexicana," *Espejo* (México), I, 1 (1967), 163-173.

Sommers, Joseph. "The Present Moment in the Mexican Novel," *Books Abroad*, XL (Summer 1966), 261-266.

Valadés, Edmundo, and Luis Leal. *La revolución y las letras*. México: Instituto Nacional de Bellas Artes, 1960.

STUDIES ON YÁÑEZ AND *The Edge of the Storm*

Campos, Julieta. "El barroquismo interior de Yáñez," in her *La imagen en el espejo*. México: U.N.A.M., 1965.

Connolly, Eileen M. "La centralidad del protagonista en *Al filo del agua*," *Revista Iberoamericana*, XXXII, 62 (July-Dec. 1966), 275-280.

Evans, Gilbert. "El mundo novelístico de Agustín Yáñez," Ph.D. Diss., Yale University, 1965.

Ezcurdia, Manuel de. "Trayectoria novelística de Agustín Yáñez," in *Memoria del Sexto Congreso del Instituto Internacional de Literatura Iberoamericana*. México: Imprenta Universitaria, 1954.

Flores Olea, Victor. "Otra vez *Al filo del agua*," *Universidad de México*, XVI (Nov. 1961), 21-22.

Haddad, Elaine. "The Structure of *Al filo del agua*," *Hispania*, XLVII, 3 (Sept. 1964), 522-529.

Martínez, José Luis. "Agustín Yáñez, novelista," *Cuadernos*, No. 80 (Jan. 1964), 85-87.

Paz, Octavio. "Novela y provincia: Agustín Yáñez," *México en la Cultura*, Lit. Supp. of *Novedades*, Sept. 4, 1961, p. 3.

Vázquez Amaral, José. "Novelística de Agustín Yáñez," in *Memoria del Octavo Congreso del Instituto Internacional de Literatura Iberoamericana*. México: Editorial Cultura, 1961.

Studies on Rulfo and *Pedro Páramo*

Blanco Aguinaga, Carlos. "Realidad y estilo de Juan Rulfo," *Revista Mexicana de Literatura*, I, 1 (1955), 59-86.

Colina, José de la. "Notas sobre Juan Rulfo," *Casa de las Américas*, (Havana), No. 26 (Oct.-Nov. 1964), 133-138.

Frenk, Mariana. *"Pedro Páramo," Universidad de México*, XV, 11 (July 1961), 18-21.

Fuentes, Carlos, "La nueva novela latinoamericana," *La Cultura en México*, No. 128, supplement to *Siempre!*, July 29, 1964, pp. 2-7 and 14-16.

Harss, Luis, and Barbara Dohmann. "Juan Rulfo, or the Souls of the Departed," in their *Into the Mainstream*. New York: Harper & Row, 1966.

Irby, James East. *La influencia de Faulkner en cuatro narradores hispanoamericanos*. México: U.N.A.M., 1956.

Leal, Luis. "La estructura de *Pedro Páramo*," *Anuario de Letras* (U.N.A.M.), IV (1964), 287-294.

Rodríguez-Alcalá, Hugo. *El arte de Juan Rulfo*. México: Instituto Nacional de Bellas Artes, 1965.

STUDIES ON FUENTES, *Where the Air is Clear* AND
The Death of Artemio Cruz

Baxandall, Lee. "An Interview with Carlos Fuentes," *Studies on the Left*, III, 1 (1962), 48-56.

Couffon, Claude. "Carlos Fuentes y la novela mexicana," *Cuadernos del Congreso por la Libertad de la Cultura*, No. 42 (May-June 1960), 67-69.

Díaz-Lastra, Alberto. "Carlos Fuentes y la revolución traicionada," *Cuadernos Hispanoamericanos*, No. 185 (May 1965), 369-375.

Fernández Retamar, Roberto. "Carlos Fuentes y la otra novela de la revolución mexicana," *Casa de las Américas* (Havana), No. 26 (Oct.-Nov., 1964), 123-128.

Harss, Luis, and Barbara Dohmann. "Carlos Fuentes, or the New Heresy," in their *Into the Mainstream*. New York: Harper & Row, 1966.

Mead, Robert G. "Carlos Fuentes, Airado Novelista Mexicano," *Hispania*, L, 2 (May 1967), 229-235.

——————. "Carlos Fuentes, Mexico's Angry Novelist," *Books Abroad*, XXXVIII (Autumn 1964), 380-382.

O'Neill, Samuel J. "Psychological-Literary Techniques in Representative Contemporary Novels of Mexico," Ph.D. Diss., University of Maryland, 1965.

Reeve, Richard. "The Narrative Technique of Carlos Fuentes: 1954-1964," Ph.D. Diss., University of Illinois, 1967.

Rodríguez Monegal, Emir. "El mundo mágico de Carlos Fuentes," *Número* (Montevideo, 2nd Series), I, 2 (July-Sept. 1963), 144-159.

——————. "Carlos Fuentes: Situación del escritor en América Latina," *Mundo Nuevo* (Paris), No. 1 (July 1966), 5-21.

Stevenson, Philip. "The Very Navel of the Star," *Mainstream*, XIV (July 1961), 42-49.

West, Anthony. "An Uncouth Grace," *The New Yorker,* Aug. 8, 1964, pp. 87-90.

—————. "The Whole of Life," *The New Yorker,* March 4, 1961, pp. 123-125.

205

INDEX

DATE DUE

JUL 10 70	OCT 2 3 1978	
JUL 2	JAN 0 8 1996	
OCT 10 70		
MAY 2 5 '71		
NOV 3 0 '71		
MAR 2 '72		
OCT 4 1973		
APR 6 1974		
MAY '7		
MAY 27 '74		
JUL 8 1974		
AUG 12 '74		
AUG 2 '74		
MAY 2 '7		
JAN 2 6 '76		
SEP 27 '76		